Michael A. Surkes has earned academic degrees, awards, and honors in psychology, philosophy, and education. His research focuses on how people develop deeply coherent sets of ideas about highly complex subjects.

For teachers, students, and other ambitious learners.

Michael A. Surkes

DEVELOPING PRACTICAL WISDOM

AUSTIN MACAULEY PUBLISHERS®
LONDON · CAMBRIDGE · NEW YORK · SHARJAH

Copyright © Michael A. Surkes 2025

All rights reserved. No part of this publication may be reproduced, distributed, or transmitted in any form or by any means, including photocopying, recording, or other electronic or mechanical methods, without the prior written permission of the publisher, except in the case of brief quotations embodied in critical reviews and certain other non-commercial uses permitted by copyright law. For permission requests, write to the publisher.

Any person who commits any unauthorized act in relation to this publication may be liable to criminal prosecution and civil claims for damages.

Ordering Information
Quantity sales: Special discounts are available on quantity purchases by corporations, associations, and others. For details, contact the publisher at the address below.

Publisher's Cataloging-in-Publication data
Surkes, Michael A.
Developing Practical Wisdom

ISBN 9798891554788 (Paperback)
ISBN 9798891554795 (Hardback)
ISBN 9798891554818 (ePub e-book)
ISBN 9798891554801 (Audiobook)

Library of Congress Control Number: 2024909972

www.austinmacauley.com/us

First Published 2025
Austin Macauley Publishers LLC
40 Wall Street, 33rd Floor, Suite 3302
New York, NY 10005
USA

mail-usa@austinmacauley.com
+1 (646) 5125767

Cover art: Some Elements of Wisdom

Table of Contents

Introduction	13
Chapter 1: Wisdom: Theory and Practice	20
Cognitive Flexibility	20
The Need for Justification	22
Beliefs and Opinions	26
Applying the Idea of 'Truth'	28
Coherence Theory	30
Cognitive Equilibrium	31
Meanings	33
Applying Objectivity in Practice	35
Applying Wisdom in Action	36
Chapter 2: Managing Our Motives	38
Self-Development	38
Commitment	39
Moral Motivation	42
Empathy	44
Unconscious Motives	45
Free Will	46
Deep Motivation to Learn	47
Self-Regulated Learning	50

Chapter 3: Thinking About Thinking 52
Cognition 52
Philosophy 54
Critical Thinking 56
Creative Thinking 59
Manifesting Higher Order Thinking in Action 61
Superstition 61
Fallacies, Cognitive Biases, and Prejudices 63

Chapter 4: Human Nature and Self-Awareness 69
Understanding People 69
Ontology – Understanding the Structure of Reality 70
Physicality 73
Consciousness 75
Understanding Human Nature 76
Characterization 78
Applying Objectivity in Practice 79
Types of Intelligence 81
Problem-Solving 83
Self-Awareness 85
Mindfulness (Presence of Mind) 87
Humanism 87

Chapter 5: Educating for Wisdom 89
Developing Wisdom 89
Complexity 91
Developing Critical Discourses 92
Early Childhood Education 95

Learning Environments	*97*
Adult Learning	*101*
Transformative Learning	*102*
Complex Dynamic Systems	*105*
Transformation for Educators	*108*
Barriers to Transformative Education	*110*
Chapter 6: Producing Self-Fulfillment	**112**
Happiness	*112*
Possibilities for Self-Development	*114*
Applying Commitment in Action	*115*
Diminishing Suffering	*117*
Self-Determinism	*119*
Taking Action	*120*
Emotions	*122*
Managing Intrapersonal Conflict	*125*
Changing Our Stories	*127*
Cultural History	*128*
Personal Stories	*129*
Peak Experience and Peak Performance	*131*
Love and Intimacy	*132*
Chapter 7: Communication and Relationship	**134**
Effective Communication	*134*
Resolving Interpersonal Conflict	*136*
Competition Vs. Cooperation	*138*
The Third Entity	*140*
Creating Progressive Dialogues	*141*

Beyond Ego	*143*
Cooperating	*145*
Ways of Communicating	*147*
Caring	*149*
Judging People	*151*
Applying Flexibility in Action	*152*
Equity	*152*
Workability: Consensus and Consent	*153*
Dealing with Antagonism	*154*
Guilt, Shame, Blame and Resentment	*155*
Social Consciousness	*159*
Acknowledgments	**165**
Notes	**166**

Introduction

Better thinking produces better living. Coherent reasoning and moral action combine to produce life's greatest prizes: self-fulfillment and social flourishing.

The following pages describe how people learn to think deeply and coherently about the world and human nature. They explain, in language that can be understood by any thoughtful reader, how our most cherished values are applied in action to produce individual and social success.

Practical wisdom is about providing optimal benefits for us and those around us.[1]

As American journalist and author Robert Wright noted, "Acting wisely reduces conflict in your life and strengthens your social relationships, and this fosters a sense of well-being."[2] Developing wisdom enables us to generate habits of thinking and behaving that are conducive to personal fulfillment and social success.

This book addresses three questions about how people develop and apply wisdom. These are: what is wisdom? How is wise thinking manifested in people's actions? How do people learn to become wiser?

Ideal values, such as *wisdom*, *flourishing*, *kindness and justice,* are abstract ideas, but that doesn't diminish their importance or their desirability. There are many other values that we may care to produce in our daily lives.

In theory, wisdom refers to ideal cognitive skills, "the ability to use your experience and knowledge to make sensible decisions or judgments."[3] In practice, it refers to the process of applying clear thinking and moral values in action to support the well-being of oneself and others.

We learn to apply wisdom in action from people who think very clearly and are committed to taking care of others as well as themselves.

It's obvious that people's actions aren't always directed by deeply coherent thinking and ethical reasoning. It might be wise to apply these methods in our lives, so why aren't they more prevalent? Most people are capable of learning to use them, but relatively few of us have had opportunities to work with very wise people long enough to learn their ways of thinking.

Wisdom is applied by producing results that are consistent with the values we intend to generate. For example, the ideal value *coherence* (or *coherency*) is "the situation in which all the parts of something fit together well."[4]

We may appreciate the importance of thinking coherently when deciding what we should do and what we should avoid doing. *Practical wisdom* entails applying critically analytical cognitive skills and moral discernment in daily life. It takes time and effort to develop these faculties; it also requires a commitment to becoming wiser.

Scholars have explained a great deal about how human mental functions and social relations operate. The narrative that follows explains how the experiences of motivation (desires, commitments, and attitudes) and cognition (thinking) operate to produce our behavior. It describes how people actually manage those processes to produce successful action. Each section of each chapter illustrates a facet of human functionality.

Experts in human development have emphasized the most essential process of growing wiser: psychological self-regulation, which includes self-evaluation and self-correction. Self-regulation is applied to manage our thinking, our feelings and our actions as we learn to produce better results over time.

Applying wisdom includes using reliable evidence, unambiguous reasoning, and ideal values to maintain well-justified sets of ideas (highly coherent perspectives). This process (which educators call *critical thinking*) enables us to make decisions that accord with our values.

In my academic career, I've seen that most university programs fail miserably in inspiring students to learn how to think deeply. Critical thinking is practically irrelevant to pre-service teacher programs and most other undergraduate or graduate studies, as students are required to focus on other topics while professors attend to research and administration.

Scholarly research has provided enough information in the past few decades to improve this situation. The references cited in this volume contain enough material for educators (from kindergarten teachers to post-graduate instructors) to produce courses on this subject.

In 1984, feminist philosopher Nel Noddings wrote, "The primary aim of all education must be nurturance of the ethical ideal."[5] Two decades ago, educational psychologist Robert Sternberg recommended that educational institutions should develop curricula that are designed to promote wisdom.[6]

Chapter 1 of the narrative describes how meanings are derived from language, and it emphasizes the importance of *operationalism*: the appropriate use of evidence in forming our opinions and making our decisions.[7] Drawing from research in science, psychology, and philosophy, this chapter explains why achieving complete certainty (indubitable truths) about complex ideas is not a practical objective. It presents the case that wisdom isn't about knowing the absolute truth about the world or its people; rather, it's about figuring out the most sensible (coherent) and beneficial (moral) ways to operate in various situations.

Chapter 2 focuses on the possibility of consciously and purposefully regulating our motives (needs, desires, urges, and intentions). It describes how we can learn to manage our behavior by clarifying (to ourselves and others) which of our objectives is more important than others at a given time. It also refers to a set of dispositions (attitudes and tendencies) that are associated with generating deep and critical thinking, including curiosity, open-mindedness, rigor, and perseverance.

Our values may be manifested as *purposes* (clearly articulated intentions), and wisdom includes the intention to apply our values in action. For example, the value of cognitive flexibility (open-mindedness) can be applied to revise our perspectives when we notice an incoherency.

In practice, we can decide to produce specific goals and then work hard to achieve them. I define the ideal value of *self-determinism* as the process of planning and enacting our activities in accordance with our declared purposes.

The third chapter elucidates the processes involved in thinking (*cognition*, to psychologists). *Critical thinking* is a set of cognitive tools for analyzing and explaining complex subjects. *Fallacies* and *biases* are described as cognitive pitfalls, common errors in reasoning.

Chapter 4 explores the philosophy of human understanding, emphasizing the crucial distinction between theories (abstractions) and practices (actions). It's a common practice to identify subjective descriptions as observable occurrences. For example, "I see two people *arguing*" reports my interpretation of what I'm observing, not the actions of the subjects. Arguing is an abstract description (an assessment or opinion) of the observable action *conversing*.

Our interpretations of events are theoretical, but we can evaluate their coherency through objective (practical) methods, including the appropriate use of evidence. It's especially useful to assess our beliefs in consultation with others who might see things differently.

Chapter 5 presents educational theories and practices associated with developing deep thinking and deep learning. In early life, we each learned a set of fundamental ideas (presumptive beliefs) from the people around us. *Accommodation* is the act of revising what one understands to produce more powerful insights into how things operate.

Chapter 6 describes individual fulfillment (contentment or life satisfaction). We each have two distinct sets of ideas about ourselves: our individual identities (how we understand ourselves to have been) and our ideal self-images (how we'd like to become). The differences between these two perspectives represent possibilities for progress.

Various disciplines have been created as contexts for intentionally producing life satisfaction.[8] Many such programs require that we develop commitments to coherency and morality.

When working with others, we can use powerful action dialogues to facilitate setting and producing ambitious goals. We can identify our past mistakes and figure out how to correct them. We can develop new and more productive methods to apply in action.

We can work intentionally to develop relationships with people who will support us in achieving our highest goals. Morality is associated with actively caring for others' needs; it's facilitated by empathy, the experience of understanding and feeling what someone else understands or feels.

Chapter 7 addresses social flourishing, the process of interacting with others in ways that are mutually satisfactory. This may require negotiation, which may succeed if nobody insists on having their own way.

Communicating is facilitated by applying the value of cooperation. It's easy to tell whether someone is cooperating or not; when people focus solely on their own concerns, mutual satisfaction is likely to be impossible.

Cognitive scientist and educator Diane Halpern has recommended that,

[H]igher education needs to be redesigned. A successful pedagogical philosophy that will serve as a basis for learning must incorporate an understanding of the way in which learners acquire and organize information. This philosophy must address how students represent knowledge internally, the way they store it (that is, keep it in their minds), the way these representations change, and the way they resist change over time.[9]

Social consciousness is associated with individual commitments to human solidarity and beneficence toward others. Educational programs may be designed to promote these values by inspiring young people to adopt lifestyles that include lifelong learning, critical analysis, and moral discernment.

Chapter 1
Wisdom: Theory and Practice

Cognitive Flexibility

Philosophers have described practical wisdom as coherent thinking that results in *moral discernment*: clear reasoning about what one should or shouldn't do in problematic situations.

To apply wisdom in practice, we must decide which actions are most likely to be optimally beneficial for everyone who is affected,[10] and then perform those actions even when the alternatives are simpler or easier.

In 2000, after spending eight years studying science and twenty years working as a computer analyst, I decided to go back to school to learn what philosophers had been saying about wisdom.

I enrolled in a course called Epistemology – the philosophy of knowing and understanding. The professor, who was ten or fifteen years older than I was, had a lively and cheerful style that I admired immediately. To begin the course, he posed a question to us (which I can't recall). He then specified two potential (conflicting) responses and asked the class which answer we preferred.

I raised my hand first, and I told him which solution I thought was better. He asked me why I thought that, and I explained my reasoning.

"That's very good," he said. "Now tell me all the reasons for believing the other answer."

My jaw muscles went slack, betraying my astonishment. What he'd suggested was practically incomprehensible to me. I stuttered, "Uh – isn't that the job for someone who believes the other side?"

"No!" he replied. "This is philosophy! To *do* philosophy we need to examine all the reasons for every answer!"

That moment revealed to me what I'd been missing in practically every argument I'd ever had. I'd been focusing on justifying what I understood and rebutting alternative ideas. As a result, I couldn't fully understand why some people thought differently than I did.

Believing that I was right had prevented me from realizing that other points of view might be equally (or even more) sensible than mine.

I soon learned that the idea of *philosophical charity* suggests that we should consider ideas that are different from ours with an open mind before rejecting them.[11] Open-mindedness (*cognitive flexibility*) enables us to examine the consequences of applying various interpretations of an idea in particular situations.

Some cognitive habits (ways of thinking) facilitate clear reasoning and progressive learning, while others are more likely to prevent us from being reasonable or learning new perspectives.

Reflective thinking (self-reflection, or *metacognition*) refers to examining, evaluating, and correcting one's own ideas. These processes are essential components of practical wisdom.

The Need for Justification

By the end of the eighteenth century, the *correspondence theory of truth* had long been a basis of the philosophical study of knowledge. That theory specifies that the word 'truth' refers to an exact correspondence between our description of an object and the object itself.

However, two hundred years ago German philosopher Immanuel Kant defined the limits of human understanding quite clearly: we can never be completely certain that our descriptions of things correspond exactly to the things themselves.

No correspondence can possibly be established between things that we can't detect and our ideas about them. If we can't observe something, then we can't verify our descriptions of that thing.

Kant's realization initiated a crisis in the field of philosophy, and its consequences were profound. He brought philosophy into line with the bourgeoning field of empirical science, which presumes that the most useful knowledge about nature is *sensory experience*: our observations of events as they occur. As described by philosophyterms.com:

Empiricism is the philosophy of knowledge by observation. It holds that the best way to gain knowledge is to see, hear, touch, or otherwise sense things directly. In stronger versions, it holds that this is the only kind of knowledge that really counts.[12]

In 1972, Karl Popper, the renowned Austrian-British philosopher of science, acknowledged that scientific principles should not be considered unquestionably true.

Only symbolic languages (arithmetic and logic) deal with confirmable truths. All else, he wrote – including

> ...the part that comprises the natural sciences, such as physics and physiology – is essentially conjectural or hypothetical in character; there are simply no sufficient reasons for holding these hypotheses to be true, let alone certainly true.[13]

As British theoretical physicist Stephen Hawking put it, "Reality is not a quality you can test with litmus paper."[14]

The only facts about the world are observations and measurements, which scientists call *data* or *evidence*. Our beliefs about what these facts *mean* are inferences (interpretations, not truths).

The implication of this perspective is clear: we shouldn't believe that our inferential beliefs are absolutely true. *Fallibilism*[15] is the idea that no belief or theory can ever be conclusively proved true – including the most widely accepted scientific claims.

Uncertainty may be difficult, awkward, embarrassing, or even painful. Nevertheless, the best that we can do is distinguish which sets of ideas are most coherent (best supported by reliable evidence and cogent reasoning).

On the other hand, it's possible to demonstrate clearly that a theory is false.

> Whenever observable evidence contradicts a theoretical relationship between events, we should understand that the theory is incorrect.

It might be difficult to accept that we can't assume beyond doubt that the sun will rise tomorrow morning.[16] It may be painful to acknowledge that people can't possibly know *for certain* the truth about scientific principles, morality, beauty, goodness, creativity, justice, politics, or religion.

Even so, we can develop our abilities to think deeply, critically, and coherently about such things.

Unfortunately, Kant's insight into the limits of human understanding has been distorted and misused as the "post-truth" era has overtaken the social and political world.[17] Contemporary society is polarized between those who understand that facts are the basis of rationality and effective communication, and those who find it more convenient to rely on imagination and deception rather than evidence and reason in their attempts to influence people.

Social and political discourse has been corrupted by the actions of politicians and pundits who ignore facts, discount reason, and clutter the public space with hateful rhetoric fueled by lies.

Kant's revelation transformed the study of philosophy, but there's never been a good reason to abandon the process of *justification* ("The action of or result of showing something to be just, right, or reasonable..."[18]). There are ways to determine which ideas are more coherent and beneficial than others; however, these methods require the cognitive skills, and the confidence, to think things through.

Many authors have made this point. For example, in *Truth: How the Many Sides to Every Story Shape Our Reality*,[19] Hector Macdonald noted that misleaders use *partial truths* (stories that seem to be more or less coherent) to convince people to think and act in particular ways. He urges readers to think carefully before deciding which stories to adopt. He wrote that we should learn to identify the numerous ways in which people manipulate meanings, and we should learn the tricks that nefarious communicators use to persuade people to do their bidding.

In *Weaponized Lies: How to Think Critically in the Post-Truth Era*, psychologist Daniel J. Levitin explained how logic and argumentation should be used to justify our opinions while warning that belief in falsehoods is a major cause of "bad, even fatal, outcomes." He noted,

> …the language that we use has begun to obscure the relationship between fact and fantasy. [T]his is a dangerous by-product of a lack of education…that has now affected an entire generation of citizens.[20]

Contemporary experts in science and philosophy now regard *coherence* ("The quality of being logically integrated, consistent, and intelligible; congruity"[21]), rather than truth, as the gold standard for human understanding. Instead of seeking the absolute truth about the world or people, we can use critical thinking and ethical reasoning to apply coherent justifications to decide which discourses (speech and texts) are more cogent than others.

> In practice, highly coherent discourses are developed and maintained by evaluating evidence and reasoning to determine which sets of ideas are better justified than others.

Subjectivity refers to the unique quality of individual experiences: they exist only in one person's mind. As American philosopher Harry Frankfurt observed, without confidence in our beliefs about the world, we have no grounding for what we should think or do.[22]

Objectivity concerns objects and actions that are observable by more than one person. This idea emphasizes the importance of applying evidence in our linguistic discourses.[23] To communicate effectively we articulate our objective justifications (evidence and reasoning) clearly so that others can comprehend, scrutinize, and evaluate them.

Certainty about our presumptive beliefs obstructs the processes of inquiry (investigation, analysis, and discovery) and learning. Thus, scientific objectivity demands that "…the claims, methods, and results of science are not, or should not be influenced by particular perspectives, value commitments, community bias or personal interests…"[24]

Historical records of observations and measurements are objective in the sense that they can be observed. However, such records represent what occurred with more or less precision. That's why professional observers are trained to inspect, measure, and record things as carefully and accurately as they possibly can. It's also why some facts are more accurate, reliable, and useful than others.

As a result of this variability, an extremely important aspect of critical analysis is judging the reliability of reports about observed phenomena.

Beliefs and Opinions

We may be quite certain about what we think or feel (our subjective experiences). However, our linguistic (objective) ideas may be inaccurate, no matter how strongly we believe them.

Of course, there are many instances where facts indicate clearly that our understandings are very well justified.

Soldiers stormed the beaches of Normandy on D-Day; Venus is nearer to the sun than Jupiter. We're *practically* certain about many things, even though we might sometimes be mistaken about some of them.

However, even a wide consensus of belief (*acclamation*) doesn't demonstrate infallibility. Everybody once agreed that the Earth is flat, which (most people now agree) is incorrect.

According to brittanica.com, *cognitive bias* refers to "systematic errors in the way individuals reason about the world due to subjective perception of reality. Cognitive biases are predictable patterns of error in how the human brain functions and therefore are widespread."[25]

As David Rock, co-founder of the NeuroLeadership Institute, points out:

> Your brain doesn't like uncertainty – it's like a type of pain, something to be avoided. Certainty, on the other hand, feels rewarding, and we tend to steer toward it, even when it might be better for us to remain uncertain.[26]

Two very common and closely related biases prevent us from noticing that we're mistaken and correcting ourselves. *Certainty bias* is the problematic tendency to think (and perhaps insist) that a belief is unquestionably true.[27] *Confirmation bias* is the common inclination to accept evidence in favor of one's own beliefs while ignoring or rejecting evidence that supports a different view.[28]

In 1807, German philosopher Georg Hegel noted that many of our individual perspectives are regarded as unquestionable:

Quite generally, the familiar, just because it is familiar, is not cognitively understood. The commonest way in which we deceive either ourselves or others about understanding is by assuming something as familiar, and accepting it on that account; with all its pros and cons, *such knowing never gets anywhere, and it knows not why.*[29]

While it might be impossible to avoid biases completely, we can learn to notice when they happen. Awareness of biases is essential if we intend to manage them; if we're aware of these common tendencies, then we can realize when they're affecting our beliefs. That realization enables us to correct ourselves.

Critical thinking (described in Chapter 3) involves guarding our reasoning very carefully against such predispositions to avoid fooling ourselves. Chapter 4 presents a list of common cognitive biases.

Applying the Idea of 'Truth'

There remain two ways in which the concept *truth* may be applied correctly to signify the accuracy of our statements.

Authenticity

Authenticity describes the action of representing our thoughts and feelings accurately to other people.[30] It's about observing our experiences clearly and *telling the truth* about what we remember, what we observe, what we think, and what we feel.

Formal Truth

As Popper noted, the "formal languages" (arithmetic and logic) use symbols to preserve truths. However, the symbols don't correspond to actual events.

For example, in formal logic:

If a=b and b=c, then a=c.

This is a logical statement with two given truths: a=b and b=c. The conclusion (a=c) is a *deductive* truth. We say that truth is *preserved*.

This relationship is purely theoretical. The symbols a, b, and c don't refer to anything in particular. The *operator* (=) defines the relationships between the variables.

We can also use regular (so-called "natural") languages in logical ways to preserve formal truths. Here's a logical statement expressed in natural language:

If a man (A) has a son (B), and B has a son (C), then A is C's grandfather.

This is logically correct (formally true) because we define the operators ("son" and "grandfather") in particular ways. *However, if we refer to actual events, logical forms can no longer account for everything. Unlike logical deduction, evidence comes into play, inferences are drawn, and absolute certainty becomes irrelevant.*

Coherence Theory

We may apply reliable evidence and logical reasoning to identify *the best available descriptions* (theories or beliefs) about the processes that we observe.

Coherence theory (*coherentism*) doesn't require that we understand the world conclusively. It stipulates that our beliefs are more or less justifiable according to the reliability of the evidence and the cogency of the reasoning upon which they're based.

To illustrate this, we can take the previous example out of the realm of formal logic and place it in the world of actual circumstances. That is, we may suppose that the following sentence applies to three living people:

John has a son (Jeff); Jeff has a son (Jim); therefore, John is Jim's grandfather.

Is John actually Jim's *biological* grandfather? Once we take our claim outside the area of logic, the first two assertions may be questioned rather than accepted as given. To demonstrate parenthood in accordance with factual evidence, we need objective justification.

Although we can't easily observe the biological connections between individuals, we can do some investigative work to infer the likelihood of these relationships.[31]

The DNA results are in! The lab techs have done repeated tests, and they've determined that Jeff is *evidently* John's son, and Jim is *evidently* Jeff's biological offspring. Now we can be *practically* certain that Jim is John's grandson. Any thoughtful person who understands the technical processes would agree. The issue is settled beyond reasonable doubt.

Of course, a reasonable conclusion is not synonymous with certainty. The samples or the lab computers might possibly have been tampered with, or the technicians might have been bribed.

Cognitive Equilibrium

To illustrate the idea of deep coherence, American philosopher John Rawls stressed the importance of continually corroborating our observations and conceptions while forming and reforming our beliefs. According to this approach, when any belief is contradicted by a reliably confirmed observation it must be modified or discarded, and all convictions which depend upon that belief for their justification must also be altered or abandoned.[32]

Applying those actions in practice enables us to produce more coherent and more complex sets of ideas over time. Rawls called his model "wide dynamic reflective equilibrium."

Of course, we can't justify all our ideas, but this idealized description indicates how we can become wiser *on purpose* through metacognitive self-correction.

The importance of cognitive flexibility and self-correction in developing wisdom has been widely recognized. For example, scientists at the forefront of research have learned to think in established patterns (*hegemonies*); these are the best theories that they know, the ones they teach to their students. These presumptive ideas define which discourses are justifiable within an area of study.[33] Practitioners who deviate from these established ways of thinking are unlikely to receive much attention from those who don't – unless they produce new evidence to justify their revolutionary views.

Science has progressed in leaps and bounds when renegade researchers have created new theories that provide more explanatory and predictive power than the previously established hegemony. When this occurs, a scientist is said to have *broken* that paradigm (see Chapter 5 on Transformative Learning).

For example, prior to the sixteenth century, scholars agreed that the Earth was at the center of the universe and that all other astronomical objects revolved around our planet. However, in 1514 Polish astronomer Nicolas Copernicus demonstrated that the observed motion of planets in our solar system contradicted that model.

Most of us now accept that the sun is positioned at the center of the solar system.

Discovering new perspectives isn't restricted to scientific research; any of us can transform our beliefs by finding more coherent and more useful ways to understand the evidence that we perceive. Self-reflection may result in altering one's ideas and producing new insights into how things operate. The act of revising what we previously understood by adopting a novel perspective is called *accommodation*.

Reconsidering our justifications is more difficult than insisting that our beliefs are true, but the former process produces a more systematic, comprehensive, and precise way of thinking. In practice, this may require a) refraining from believing that anyone has access to the absolute truth about the world or the people in it, and b) listening carefully and openly to other people's ideas with the intention to compare and resolve alternative perspectives.

If we're not clear about which ideas on a subject are most coherent, we may rely on a *consensus of experts* to indicate the best discourses on that topic. If top experts disagree, then there's no way for the rest of us to decide which perspective is most cogent.

Meanings

Linguistic artifacts (words, sentences, stories etc.) connote different things to different people. To begin to understand how thinking and learning operate, it's useful to recognize how linguistic meanings emerge in our thinking.

Abstract (intangible) ideas (such as *wisdom* or *justice*) are generally described as social (or linguistic) *constructs* because they don't refer to things that can be directly observed or measured (such as lights or sounds).[34] So, how do we understand what abstract ideas mean?

To summarize more than a century of philosophical research into that question: *meaning is determined by social usage*[35] – how ideas were used by the people who taught them to us. Austrian-British philosopher Ludwig Wittgenstein produced that explanation in the 1960s, and philosophers of language have widely agreed on this perspective.[36]

For example, we learn that the words *right* and *wrong* refer to things that should or shouldn't be done. Of course, learning what words mean doesn't guarantee that we'll use them very coherently or very effectively!

Language is said to be objective because it consists of observable things (symbols and sounds) that can be perceived by more than one person. In contrast, understanding is an individual subjective experience.

To maintain coherent reasoning, it's essential to recognize the distinction between objective knowledge (linguistic meanings) and subjective knowledge (experiences of knowing). Popper emphasized this fundamental perspective, writing that we must:

…distinguish sharply between *knowledge in the subjective sense and knowledge in the objective sense*…Knowledge in the objective sense consists *not* of *thought processes* but of *thought contents*. It consists…of that content which can be, at least approximately, translated from one language into another.[37]

For example, the word *meaning* itself has two completely different definitions. It signifies either a) a *definition* (objective linguistic knowledge) or b) a subjective *interpretation*. Definitions are publicly observable, but interpretations are subjective experiences that are based on our previous understandings of how words have been used (a process that underlies our conscious thoughts).

Our interpretations are firmly established in our thinking; we rarely need to consider them since our attention is usually on more practical concerns (making a point, producing a result, influencing people, etc.).

If we don't distinguish personal (subjective) perspectives from public (objective) knowledge, then it's not possible to apply objectivity in practice. Without applying this distinction in conversation with others, there's no basis for consensus about what abstract objects *are* and there's no basis for agreement on what they *mean*.

British philosopher John Locke realized this in the seventeenth century:

We should have a great many fewer disputes in the world, if words were taken for what they are, the signs of our ideas only; and not for things themselves. For, when we argue about matter, or any the like term, we truly argue only about the idea we express by that sound, whether that precise idea agree to anything really existing in nature or no. And if men would tell what ideas they make their words stand for, there could not be half that obscurity or wrangling in the search or support of truth that there is.[38]

Applying Objectivity in Practice

Many scholars have emphasized the philosophical importance of distinguishing objective (publicly observable) things from our subjective beliefs, theories, and opinions about them.

In the late nineteenth and early twentieth centuries, a group of American philosophers[39] developed a new philosophical tradition called *philosophical pragmatism,* which describes the relative usefulness of various definitions and interpretations. They understood that *meanings cannot be clarified unless they pertain to some form of observable action.*[40]

Operationalism refers to the application of this principle in action.[41] Scientists apply operationalism through the process of measurement to collect data (factual evidence) that they use to develop highly coherent inferences about the natural world.

We don't need to be scientists to do that. Operationalism is also suitable for resolving interpersonal conflicts about our ideas and interpretations; it provides tools for understanding each other's meanings. To comprehend each other's ideas clearly, we may apply objective definitions and operational measures in our conversations.

For example, if I criticize a neighbor for playing music *too loudly*, I'm not discussing the music's actual (measurable) volume; I'm referring to my *opinion* about it. I'd be mistaken to believe that I was referring to the noise itself unless I'd used a properly calibrated sound meter to produce an operational assessment of volume. That's why cities enact laws to decide how many decibels constitute a noise infraction.

Applying Wisdom in Action

It's possible to learn new perspectives, adopt new habits, and alter our lifestyles if that's what we need to do to produce greater success for ourselves and those around us.

We can examine our habits of thought and evaluate our tendencies to behave in particular ways. We can compare what we've known and done with alternative ways of thinking and behaving. We can apply morality to figure out what should be done by discussing with others how moral values have been (or should be) interpreted in particular situations.

We're all different from each other in many ways, but we share the same types of experiences: better ideas, poorer ideas, better feelings, worse feelings, better behavior, and…well, we've all made mistakes. We also have the following in common: we each experience the same thoughts and feelings that we've experienced before; over and over, and over again, day after day, and year after year.

To succeed in life as well as we can, we need to ascertain *as we go along* that our actions are having beneficial effects – to see whether they're producing (or are likely to produce) optimal or sub-optimal results.

Consequentialism is an ethical theory which demands that we consider the likely consequences of our actions before we perform them. This process is only effective when we're aware of which outcomes are most desirable for the people around us.

Continual evaluations of what's happening and what's likely to happen inform us about what to do next. People who value morality and its instrumental (subsidiary) values (such as compassion, justice, and responsibility) can engage with each other in ethical inquiries whenever they need to figure out which actions are more likely to provide optimal benefits for people.

Scholars have elucidated the sources of human motivation, explained how people generate critical analyses, and discussed how we produce effective action by applying ethical guidelines, cooperative communication, and value-based decision-making. We can adopt these methods to apply our most precious values in practice and to accomplish our most important objectives in life.

Chapter 2
Managing Our Motives

Self-Development

Our desires and our needs are experiences that direct our actions. These *intrinsic motives* (or *drives*) move us to seek (want) some things and avoid (fear or detest) some others.

We're not necessarily stuck at our current levels of psychological development. If we notice that we want to change our historical habits of thinking and reacting, we can decide to learn new ways of thinking and more effective methods of managing ourselves.

Our motives result from our thoughts and feelings. Those experiences combine to produce our attitudes (moods or *dispositions*), which compel us to behave in certain ways.

Psychological self-regulation refers to a set of cognitive techniques that are associated with managing our ideas, our motives, and our mental reflexes.

As described in Chapter 1, *metacognitive self-regulation* (self-reflection) refers to a set of cognitive practices which, applied in combination, are essential for producing highly coherent beliefs and opinions: *self-observation* is the process of monitoring what we think, *self-evaluation* is about reconsidering those ideas to check for errors in our reasoning, and *self-correction* is the practice of revising our beliefs by correcting our ideas when errors are found.

Just as we can focus on learning different ways of thinking, we can also work to alter our emotional and motivational mechanisms. *Affective self-regulation* (also called emotion regulation or *metamotivation*[42]) is about managing our needs, feelings, desires, and attitudes.

Overall, the evidence suggests that metamotivation is an important factor in determining success in life, and that interventions designed to promote metamotivation could be effective in helping individuals to achieve their goals.[43]

We're not necessarily stuck with our old ways of thinking and feeling. It takes work to learn to understand how our cognitive and motivational functions direct our thoughts, feelings and actions, but the most effective way to improve our lives is to take charge of these processes and modify them on purpose.

Cognitive and affective self-development take time and effort, but the result (increasing self-determinism, fulfilment and flourishing) is worth the effort.

Commitment

We experience many transient desires; sometimes we want one thing, sometimes another. Self-determinism (the possibility of articulating and fulfilling one's highest purposes in life) is manifested in action through *self-determination* (usually called simply "determination").[44] We apply determination wisely when we make well-justified decisions about what we should do and when we should do it.

We must fulfil our most basic (biological) needs to survive. We also have *psychological* (learned) needs that are based on what we understand we ought to do. For example, I might need to talk to a friend about my problems, and I definitely need to maintain my car on a regular schedule.

In 1971, American philosopher Harry Frankfurt described the possibility of managing our motives. He suggested that we can *rank our desires* in terms of their relative importance.[45] By deciding that *some desires are more desirable than others*, we can arrange them in a hierarchy of *higher-* and *lower-order desires*.

Some desires are clearly more important than others when it comes to enacting our values. Frankfurt called our higher-ranking (most valued) aspirations *commitments*.

> We apply our commitments in practice by sharing them with others who will encourage and support us, and by setting and achieving goals that manifest those values in action. Rather than being diverted from one situation to another by our instincts, we can manage to focus on accomplishing specific goals associated with our most important ideals.

We make value-based decisions by considering what should and shouldn't be done in each situation. Applying metamotivation involves weighing our commitments in each context, fulfilling them as much as we can, and indulging in less vital activities on fewer occasions. To apply the values of *diligence* and *productivity* in action, we disregard transient urges to accomplish more essential goals.

For example, the value of *health* refers to the purpose of maintaining a healthy body, and it implies the application of several instrumental values in practice, including *exercise*, *nutrition,* and *safety*. The desire to exercise regularly, eat nutritious foods, and stay safe is clearly much more important to maintaining our health than any desire we might have to avoid exercise, eat junk food, or run across a busy highway.

This may be obvious if we think about it, but many people have severe difficulties with their health due to their failure to apply those values in practice.

An *intention* is a *purpose*: the result of a *decision* about the importance of a particular value. For example, I make sure that my car is roadworthy because I've decided to apply the value of *safety* in my life. My intention to share my situation with others is based on my decisions about the values of *relationship* and *communication.*

Values are abstract; but in practice we fulfill our purposes intentionally by setting and accomplishing specific goals. Talking with friends and maintaining my car's brakes are examples of applying relationship and safety in action.

A *tendency* is a historical record of behavioral habits.[46] To produce better results, we can adopt better habits. We can learn to manage and improve (supersede or fine-tune) our habitual beliefs, attitudes, tendencies, and behaviors.

Planning is a key value to be applied in any complex project.[47] That's how people accomplish the most difficult objectives, such as winning world championships, completing difficult negotiations to reach an agreement with someone (despite the frustration that may accompany such efforts), or creating new enterprises even though they fear the risks.

We apply self-determinism in practice by setting ambitious goals for ourselves and then accomplishing them. This may include seeking the advice of experts who can support us in learning to do what we haven't done before.

To apply self-determinism effectively, we must consider the short- and long-term consequences of our actions.

Moral Motivation

The ideal of *the good life* would probably look different to each of us, but we can each apply metamotivation to make our lives better and better.

In the fourth century BC, Aristotle described an ideal human lifestyle (*eudaimonia*) as "an activity of the soul in conformity with excellence or virtue."[48] He also described practical wisdom *(phrónēsis)* as the rational consideration of human functions with the purpose of deciding what we ought to do.[49]

Practical wisdom requires that one appreciates the value of morality and is committed to applying it in action.

> To work well with others, we may discuss the consequences of our intentions and our actions with our social partners, create consensual agreements about what people ought to do, and apply those agreements in practice.

In addition to his work on denoting the limits of human understanding, Kant also described the idea of *moral will* (or moral responsibility): the intention to apply morality in practice. He called this concept *good will*.[50] It signifies a commitment to take care of others as well as oneself.

We can use the tools of morality (ethical discourses) to resolve tough questions about what we ought to do. For example, consequentialism requires that we figure out what's best by balancing the benefits and harms that are likely to result from behaving in particular ways. Of course, this task may be problematic, since we can't predict all the potential consequences of our actions.

In theory, the onus falls on each of us to decide which actions or activities are likely to produce the most benefits in each situation – that is, to apply moral discernment. In practice, we can carefully consider the potential consequences of alternative actions to decide which outcomes we should produce and how we should produce them. We may consult with others during this process.

We develop wisdom as we consider and reconsider the reasons for deciding to do one thing rather than another. A commitment to self-reflection develops over time as we learn to make decisions based on beneficent values in accordance with presumptive ethical guidelines (such as caring, consequentialism, and virtue).

Practical wisdom isn't rule-based; it refers to producing cogent analyses of moral issues and their contexts. Ethical values, such as benevolence and justice, provide overarching guidelines for producing moral assessments based on analyzing dynamic situations (rather than applying rules without considering contextual factors). Progressive ethical discourses consist of thoughtful dialogues that are designed to decide what's best for people in particular circumstances.

If one doesn't care much about other people's needs, then one's actions will demonstrate relatively low moral responsibility – whether one claims to have moral motives or not.

Empathy

Applying wisdom in action requires generating and applying empathy.

Empathy means experiencing someone else's experience; it's an aspect of social intelligence.[51] It may be defined as "the psychological identification with or vicarious experiencing of the feelings, thoughts, or attitudes of another."[52]

We get along better with our social partners when we clearly understand their beliefs and desires; we're then better equipped to make mutually beneficial decisions. We can hardly consider the consequences of our actions if we don't understand what others think and feel about what we do or what we propose to do.

On the other hand, as noted by Barry Schwartz and Kenneth Sharpe in *Practical Wisdom: The Right Way to Do the Right Thing,* we should understand that people's feelings should not be the primary focus of moral consideration. That place should be occupied by moral reasoning.

Reason enables people to decide whether a given action was good or bad – right or wrong. Emotions kick in only after the evaluation is done…Emotion…is not so much the ally of reason as a spectator… Its proper place is *not* to interfere with moral choice making. [53]

Unconscious Motives

Everything that we do is driven by some motive or other, but we're not always aware of the reasons for our actions. Even if we think of one, there may be others lurking in the cognitive background.

Occasionally, we realize that we've acted in a way we shouldn't. If morality is important to us, and our actions produced damage to property or harm to another person, then we should do our best to repair any damage we've done and to make amends to people who were adversely affected.

If we intend to avoid making the same mistakes over and over, it's especially useful to understand what drives us to react badly.

> We can examine the thoughts and feelings that *immediately preceded* the actions we're concerned about; those experiences drove us to express ourselves without consideration of the consequences. This awareness enables us to learn to react differently.

We've all suffered grief, misery, frustration, anger, hatred, fear, shame, regret, disgust, despair, anxiety, and helplessness. When we experience these emotions, it's natural to want to escape them. We may fear or be ashamed of our feelings, but repressing or denying them may drive us to do something counterproductive or harmful.[54]

We can learn to deal with our worst thoughts and feelings rather than denying or repressing them. We can diminish their impact by engaging in self-discovery and self-regulation. We might engage in psychotherapy, or we might discuss our difficulties with other supportive partners who can advise us about how to manage our emotional issues.

Free Will

Can one's *will* ever be unconstrained? Questions about freedom of decision (*free will*) have puzzled people for ages and continue to do so.

Can we ever make a decision that isn't fully determined by automatic mental processes? It may seem that there are only two options: either we can occasionally make decisions without constraint (free will), or else we're always involuntarily driven to think what we think and do what we do (a theory called *hard determinism*).

There's no evidence that free will refers to anything other than itself; it's an intangible linguistic construct without any operational basis. On the other hand, determinism (cause and effect) is ubiquitous.[55] Yet, *disbelieving* in freedom of choice may seem to be a repugnant prospect.

Philosopher Steven Cave reviewed experimental research which seems to indicate that *people who believe that their choices are unconstrained behave more morally than those who don't*.

It seems that when people stop believing they are free agents, they stop seeing themselves as blameworthy for their actions. Consequently, they act less responsibly and give in to their baser instincts.[56]

Given these results, Cave suggested that it might be better for everyone if we all believed in freedom of decision.

It seems to me that (while many of our decisions are made automatically without any consideration whatsoever) some of our decision-making processes are less constrained than others.

I can't decide to do something that I've never thought about; I must be aware of a possibility for action before I can decide to enact it.

Also, it seems that the better we understand how the world (and people) operate, the more aware we can be about the nature of our circumstances, and *the more options we might conceive for effective action*.

Thus, some decisions seem to be less constrained than others.

> The scope of our cognitive perspectives limits the potential choices we may consider; our decisions are more or less constrained by how well we understand our situations. The limits of one's free will may be understood as the extent to which one's learning history provides insights into prospective alternatives for action.

Deep Motivation to Learn

If a powerful desire occurs very often, it results in a strong tendency to behave in particular ways.

With regard to the desire for cognitive self-development, there are many attitudes and tendencies that facilitate deep thinking and deep learning. We may develop those motives and habits intentionally. We can learn what they are, and we can manage to apply them on purpose.[57]

Some people feel that they've completed their education. They went to school, became physically mature, and are well settled into a lifestyle. They may think that they're smarter (and/or wiser) than most people they meet. It's unlikely for them to add studying complex abstract ideas to their usual hobbies.

Some of us are actively learning about ourselves and the world we're enmeshed in. *Lifelong learning* is the possibility of maintaining a commitment to self-development throughout one's lifetime, educating ourselves whenever we have an opportunity, with the possibility of deciding specifically what we want to learn and how we want to learn it.

Learning to become wiser every day is one possibility that we can imagine and pursue. Many educators are doing their best to promote the value of doing so.

In 1988, on behalf of the American Philosophical Association, philosopher Peter Facione convened a panel of forty-six highly experienced educators to conduct a collaborative study of educational applications of critical thinking. Two years later, they produced a list of *critical thinking dispositions* – a set of attitudes associated with developing well-justified sets of ideas (Table 1).[58] We may demonstrate these tendencies to various degrees at various times.

Approaches to life and living in general:
Inquisitiveness with regard to a wide range of issues
Concern to become and remain generally well-informed
Alertness to opportunities to use CT [critical thinking]
Trust in the processes of reasoned inquiry
Self-confidence in one's own ability to reason
Open-mindedness regarding divergent world views
Flexibility in considering alternatives and opinions
Understanding of the opinions of other people
Fair-mindedness in appraising reasoning
Honesty in facing one's own biases, prejudices, stereotypes, egocentric or socio-centric tendencies
Prudence in suspending, making, or altering judgments
Willingness to reconsider and revise views where honest reflection suggests that change is warranted
Approaches to specific issues, questions, or problems:
Clarity in stating the question or concern
Orderliness in working with complexity
Diligence in seeking relevant information
Reasonableness in selecting and applying criteria
Care in focusing attention on the concern at hand
Persistence though difficulties are encountered
Precision to the degree permitted by the subject and the circumstance

Table 1. Critical thinking dispositions

According to the author of the panel's report,

> The ideal critical thinker is habitually inquisitive, well-informed, trustful of reason, open-minded, flexible, fair-minded in evaluation, honest in facing personal biases, prudent in making judgments, willing to reconsider…diligent in seeking relevant information, reasonable in the selection of criteria, focused in inquiry, and persistent in seeking results which are as precise as the subject and the circumstances of inquiry permit. Thus, educating good critical thinkers means working toward this ideal.[59]

This hypothetical description may serve as an inspiration for those who intend to develop deeply coherent sets of ideas about complex issues.

Self-Regulated Learning

Educational psychology is the study of how people learn and how educators can support people in learning. In practice, learning is facilitated by exploring other people's beliefs, participating in unfamiliar social environments, and working with supportive mentors.

We might want to learn how to create more fulfilling lives for ourselves or to support other people more effectively. *Self-regulated learning* refers to applying effective methods for producing one's own cognitive development.[60]

Changing our ideas, attitudes, and habits *on purpose* requires intentional self-development through self-directed and self-regulated learning.

Sometimes, we need to adapt to unforeseen circumstances. We might be forced to change our habitual lifestyles and learn to navigate new ones; for example, someone who's always been wealthy might encounter financial disaster and become penniless, or someone who's always been destitute might find a lottery ticket and win millions.

Mental fitness is analogous to physical fitness. Some of us are strongly motivated to exercise our bodies and manage our nutrition, while others rarely exercise and tend to eat whatever tastes good. Clear thinking requires that we habitually exercise our mental powers and feed our minds with fresh information, as some of our cognitive powers may degrade over time if we don't exercise them.[61]

Chapter 3
Thinking About Thinking

Cognition

Philosophers have discussed knowing and understanding for millennia, and cognitive processes have been studied by a host of psychologists in the past hundred years.

This chapter focuses on the possibility of developing highly coherent sets of beliefs. It describes numerous ways (styles, or habits) of thinking, cognitive patterns that produce different types of behavior.

We each maintain a finite set of beliefs, opinions, and theories that direct our actions, but we rarely need to reconsider our perspectives, so we usually operate without much self-reflection.

Thinking is mostly automatic for human beings, but understanding cognitive functionality (our own or other people's) only becomes automatic after a period of intentional study and practice. It takes more than a little time to develop our metacognitive skills; practice is required before self-observation, self-evaluation and self-correction become habitual.[62]

How we think (our cognitive styles) is more relevant to developing deep wisdom than *what* we think. For example, as described in previous chapters, open-mindedness (thinking flexibly) facilitates the process of correcting mistaken beliefs and learning new ones. Also (while thinking quickly may sometimes be necessary), reacting quickly (automatically) to what happens around us may sometimes be less rewarding than taking a moment to reflect on what we ought to say or do.

How we think is determined by our beliefs and our values. For example, if we value *originality* more than we appreciate *tradition*, we'll be more open-minded than those who prefer a strong attachment to historical customs.

Our individual learning histories, developed over years of experience, produce our behavioral patterns. Our values determine our motives and our decisions. If one is deeply concerned with personal *safety* (avoiding risks), then one is more likely to choose gardening as a career rather than firefighting. I might be more interested in social work than in acquiring wealth (or vice versa); in either case my actions will reflect my commitments.

We all tend to favor our own beliefs over the potential alternatives. As britannica.com describes confirmation bias, "People are especially likely to process information to support their own beliefs when an issue is highly important or self-relevant."[63]

Some people enjoy thinking deeply about many issues, while others prefer to keep things simple. Some believe that it's essential to maintain coherence by paying close attention to evidence and reasoning; others prefer to believe whichever ideas they happen to like.

It's possible to insist that what we know is absolutely correct. Maintaining our beliefs might sometimes be more important than learning to modify our least coherent or least moral ideas.

If we believe that what we know is certainly true, then our views aren't subject to reconsideration. As noted in Chapter 1, certainty bias is applied by declining to consider alternative perspectives.

Someone who's committed to applying morality in action will see their desires in a different light than those who are primarily interested in their own gratification. If one thinks that social responsibility and morality are of primary importance in one's life, then one will spend more cognitive energy considering other people's needs than someone who doesn't appreciate those ideals.

We're each familiar with our own ways of figuring things out; however, if we realize that some of our cognitive habits have been counterproductive then we could decide to learn some new ones.

Analyzing linguistic knowledge enables us to determine which discourses are more coherent and more beneficial than others on the same subject. We can benefit from learning to describe various complex issues as clearly as we can, especially if we're not already well versed in a subject that's relevant to our (current or future) well-being.

The following three sections describe some subjects that scholars have found to be very useful for developing deeply coherent discourses: philosophical thinking, critical thinking, and creativity.

Philosophy

Philosophy is the study of wisdom.[64] It's applied to determine which linguistic perspectives are more reasonable (and thus more useful) than others. In other words, a philosopher's work is to distinguish which sets of ideas are *wiser* than others.

Applying philosophical thinking (by examining subjects from various perspectives and then comparing the coherence of alternative views) may contribute greatly to determining how well we succeed in the world.

Ethics is the philosophical study of morality; epistemology is research on knowledge and understanding. We can apply moral values (such as consequentialism and caring) to determine which actions are better for people in various circumstances, and we can use critical thinking (described in the next section of this chapter) to understand which cognitive perspectives (sets of ideas) are deeply coherent.

> Philosophy scholars systematically study a variety of subjects, including knowledge itself (*epistemology*). Epistemologists discuss which language specifies the best ways that we can know things, and they also point out which beliefs about knowledge prevent us from applying logic and reasoning in effective ways.

Philosophical discussions may be highly abstract, and scholars often use technical language (which may be incomprehensible to those who haven't studied academic literature on the subject). On the other hand, each of us has already formed our own perspectives on knowledge and understanding, as well as morality, politics, and education. Our personal philosophies include our views on how people ought to think, speak, and behave.

Reflective reconsideration is applied to learn how to produce better results, more satisfaction, and social benefits. The practice of *philosophical counseling* has been designed to support people in examining the qualities of our experiences and our actions, considering our alternatives, and changing our minds when it's sensible to do so.[65]

Critical Thinking

It takes time and effort to develop deep reasoning about any complex subject.

In 1987, American educational psychologist Robert Ennis defined *critical thinking* as "reasonable reflective thinking that is focused on deciding what to believe or do."[66] This concept represents a set of *methods* for figuring things out by analyzing various opinions according to observed evidence and cogent reasoning. It describes a set of cognitive and discursive processes (skills, or practices), which have been expounded at length by experts in psychology and philosophy.

Critical thinking enables us to determine whether the ideas that we apply in practice are well justified (compared with other perspectives).[67] This means overcoming certainty bias and confirmation bias by being alert for evidence and reasons which invalidate our beliefs or opinions, and conscientiously correcting ourselves when we find that we've been mistaken.

Peter Facione's study panel of forty-two philosophers and psychologists listed a set of cognitive processes and sub-processes (*skills* and *sub-skills*) that enable people to develop deeply coherent sets of ideas (Table 2).[68]

COGNITIVE SKILLS AND SUB-SKILLS

1. **Interpretation**: Categorization, Decoding Significance, Clarifying Meaning
2. **Analysis**: Examining Ideas, Identifying Arguments, Analyzing Arguments
3. **Evaluation**: Assessing Claims, Assessing Arguments
4. **Inference**: Querying Evidence, Conjecturing Alternatives, Drawing Conclusions
5. **Explanation**: Stating Results, Justifying Procedures, Presenting Arguments
6. **Self-Regulation**: Self-examination, Self-correction

Table 2. From Facione (1990).

To engage in deep thinking, we must analyze and evaluate ideas in relation to one another. How is an assertion justified? Which reliable evidence is relevant to that process? Which interpretations and arguments are more reasonable than others?

Interpretation, as described in Chapter 1, is the process of deriving meanings. We categorize (conceptualize) things by identifying what they are. For example, an *element* is a substance, a *house* is a building; a *numismatist* is a person. Those are simple things to identify, but some ideas are more complicated; for example, a *statement* might be seen as a conjecture, an insult, or a compliment.

Categorization is usually an automatic cognitive process, but when it comes to deep thinking, we should be aware that a) things aren't always what they seem, and b) things might be perceived and categorized in different (more or less reasonable) ways by different people, or even by the same person under different circumstances.

Interpretation may be quite automatic, but meanings aren't necessarily static. We may sometimes need to consider different potential meanings of what people say to clarify which interpretation seems most reasonable.

Analysis refers to breaking discourses into their component parts to examine each detail for coherency.

An *argument* is "a reason given for or against a matter under discussion…intended to convince or persuade."[69] We analyze arguments to see whether they make sense according to objective knowledge. Is the Earth flat? It may look that way, but things aren't always what they seem, so that's not a compelling argument; better evidence indicates otherwise.

Inference is the process of figuring out the implications of a claim. Alternative interpretations provide different inferences. (For example: My daughter was caught speeding; does she have a habit of being reckless, or was she momentarily distracted?)

Explanation is a description of the preceding processes and their results, which is constructed to indicate why it's more reasonable to favor one perspective rather than another.

Self-regulation (metacognition) is crucial to manifesting critical thinking in practice.

These six processes aren't sequential: they're *iterative*. This means that we identify the most coherent interpretations and explanations by repeating these techniques (in no particular sequence) during the process of considering an issue and its related contexts.

Interpretations (*connotations*) are the inputs to critical (analytical) thinking processes; explanations are the outcomes. At the end of an inquiry, we've used our experience to figure out which parts of a discourse consist of sensible language, and which sentences are less comprehensible. We've examined alternative perspectives by breaking down the meanings of the ideas, assessing the evidence and analyzing the arguments. We can then express what we've figured out and how we figured it out.

As the highly celebrated American philosopher John Dewey warned, "[A]n act of controlled inquiry demands a rich background and a disciplined insight."[70] Experts in critical thinking can evaluate the use of practices such as referral to reliable and relevant evidence, use of logical argumentation, and consideration of alternative viewpoints.[71]

Philosophical analyst Sydney Hook described how this is done:

Primarily by the clarification of meanings – a process in which their contexts are laid bare, their operational correspondences established, their implications and consistencies explored, their obscurities and ambiguities reduced…This is particularly true of the terms that are called basic or fundamental in special modes of inquiry, and of almost all terms which express evaluations and appraisals.[72]

Creative Thinking

According to Harvard University psychologist Teresa Amabile, "A product or response will be judged as creative to the extent that (a) it is both novel and appropriate, useful, correct or valuable…and (b) the task is heuristic rather than algorithmic."[73]

According to sciencedirect.com,

> Heuristics are approximate strategies or "rules of thumb" for decision-making and problem-solving that do not guarantee a correct solution but that typically yield a reasonable solution or bring one closer to hand.[74]

Amabile doesn't focus on distinguishing creative thought processes from critical thinking; instead, she describes "creativity-relevant skills," which include "breaking perceptual set" (seeing things in unusual ways), "breaking cognitive set" (thinking in different directions), understanding complexities, keeping response options open, suspending judgment, using wide (inclusive, rather than exclusive) categories for various bits of information, and remembering accurately.

British cognitivist Margaret Boden noted that original thinking refers to something that *could not have been produced before it arose*. Before any original notion can arise in anyone's thinking, one must alter something in the "system" that generates one's ideas.[75]

> A merely novel idea is one that can be described and/or produced by the same set of generative rules as are other, familiar, ideas. A genuinely original or radically creative idea is one that cannot...[T]he ascription of creativity always involves tacit or explicit reference to some specific generative system.[76]

Boden's dynamic explanation of creative processes represents the evolution and transformation of *conceptual spaces*. It describes a shift in one's perspectives, the result of *cognitive plasticity*: the willingness to re-arrange one's constitutive (generative) principles to produce novel perspectives.

Manifesting Higher Order Thinking in Action

I describe *higher order thinking* as the development of deeply coherent sets of ideas about complex phenomena.

Contemporary scholars have described how critical thinking combines cognitive skills and critical attitudes. However, our ideas are relatively useless unless they're applied in action.

Chapter 6 contains a section on action dialogues and specific conversational techniques that facilitate cooperative communication and collaborative action.

The final two sections of this chapter describe erroneous ways of thinking that are inimical to justifiable reasoning. Understanding these cognitive pitfalls and recognizing them in practice enables us a) to avoid applying faulty reasoning and b) to recognize when others make these mistakes.

Superstition

The idea *superstition* refers to a belief or assertion that's unjustifiable due to a lack of reliable supporting evidence. Examples are claims that some numbers are lucky (or unlucky), and that Santa Claus is a character who delivers gifts from a reindeer-drawn flying vehicle one day a year.

A very popular (and important) superstition holds that God is comprehensible to human beings.

To me, Santa Claus represents a very successful practical joke. Parents understand that Santa is a myth, but some want their children to believe in it because (I suppose) it increases the joy of celebrating Christmas.

I presume that many people teach their children that we shouldn't lie or mislead people, even as they manifest the illusion of Santa in their children's lives. It seems to me that this behavior might be seen as hypocritical.

As for the belief that the Ruler of the Universe has been accurately channeled through prophets who have each produced unquestionable (but quite different) Holy Scriptures: even if that were the case and a Deity actually selected those people to deliver messages, it seems impossible to determine which scriptures should be believed.

Some of us believe that the Creator is beyond human comprehension. One view holds that the universe *itself* is a Higher Power which may be called *God* or *Nature*. *Pantheism* is the belief that we can't distinguish the ideas *God* and *Universe*.[77]

These two ideas are both defined as all-encompassing. Yet, *everything* is a singular and unique concept. There can only be one example of that idea (which refers only to itself). It's also been called *reality, existence, world, multiverse* and *cosmos.*

Whatever we might call it, it seems unlikely that human consciousness could grasp the true details of *everything.*

> The belief that people can understand the ultimate truth about abstract (unobservable) things may be the most widespread superstition in human history.

Fallacies, Cognitive Biases, and Prejudices

A *fallacy* is a failed justification, a botched attempt at reasoning. According to oxforddictionaries.com, it refers to a "mistaken belief, especially one based on unsound arguments."[78]

There are many deeply nefarious ways to use language. Some people may be willing to say anything that they can imagine to demonstrate that they're right and to win arguments. People might even use fallacious arguments on purpose to win arguments by any means available.

> Understanding fallacies enables us to avoid using them and to avoid being tricked by other people's incoherent reasoning.

The following are some common examples of these misleading uses of language:

Black/White Fallacy or False Dilemma

This refers to the inappropriate (oversimplified) usage of *dichotomous* (either/or) descriptions when quantitative evaluations (*more* or *less*) are appropriate. The use of categorical adjectives may be seen as hyperbole (extreme exaggeration).

For example: Ellen is a good person. The adjective '*good*' may be measured in many ways, but the idea that anybody (or anything) is completely good is nonsensical. People are *more or less* good according to any operational measure we'd care to apply.

Ad Hominem (Personal Remarks)

A person's reasoning is completely distinct from one's personality or origins. Arguments should *not* address personalities or personal histories; only relevant evidence and objective reasoning should be used.

For example, "Ted is ignorant." "Jill is from England, so she doesn't know American history."

False Cause

If one event follows another, then it may be inappropriate to infer that the first event necessarily caused the second. A different event might have produced both results in sequence.

Jumping to Conclusions

It's essential to explore various alternatives before making important decisions.

> It is not always a mistake to make a quick decision, but when we draw a conclusion without taking the trouble to acquire enough of the relevant evidence, our reasoning uses the fallacy of jumping to conclusions…[79]

Appeal to Consequence

This is the claim that believing in something is too unpleasant to contemplate. For example, "John couldn't have said what you think you overheard – he'd never leave me for another woman!"

Cognitive biases are tendencies to think in particular erroneous ways. Like fallacies, these thinking habits produce errors in reasoning, and we're unaware of them until we learn what they are.

Biases differ from fallacies because they're not linguistic forms, so they're not directly evident in our discourses. However, research in cognitive psychology has demonstrated quite clearly how they affect our thinking.[80]

Biases often represent what we'd like to think, rather than objectively reasonable ideas.[81] As experts at the Interaction Research Foundations have warned, cognitive biases "lead to judgment and decision-making that *deviates* from rational objectivity."[82] As described previously, certainty bias and confirmation bias indicate that we tend to think very highly of our own beliefs or opinions.

Psychologists Justin Kruger and David Dunning demonstrated through careful research that most of us also tend to overestimate our abilities to perform unfamiliar tasks.

Mark Murphy, the founder of Leadership IQ, explained that the "Dunning-Kruger Effect" is a cognitive bias whereby people who are asked to predict their performance on a novel assignment tend to overestimate their ability to accomplish it. As Kruger and Dunning noted,

Not only do these people reach erroneous conclusions and make unfortunate choices, but their incompetence robs them of the metacognitive ability to realize it. Across four studies, [we] found that participants scoring in the bottom quartile on tests of humor, grammar, and logic grossly overestimated their test performance and ability…Several analyses linked this miscalibration to deficits in metacognitive skill, or the capacity to distinguish accuracy from error. Paradoxically, improving the skills of participants, and thus increasing their metacognitive competence, helped them recognize the limitations of their abilities.[83]

Here are some other common biases:

Self-Serving Bias

"The propensity to attribute positive outcomes to skill and negative outcomes to luck. In other words, we attribute the cause of something to whatever is in our own best interest. Many of us can recall times that we've done something and decided that if everything is going to plan, it's due to skill, and if things go the other way, then it's just bad luck."[84]

Hindsight Bias

"…the theory that when people predict a correct outcome, they wrongly believe that they 'knew it all along'."[85]

False Consensus Effect

"The tendency to overestimate how much other people agree with you."[86]

Optimism Bias

"Leads you to believe that you are less likely to suffer from misfortune and more likely to attain success than your peers."[87]

Anchoring Bias

"The tendency to rely too heavily on the very first piece of information you learn. If you learn the average price for a car is a certain value, you will think any amount below that is a good deal. You can use this bias to set the expectations of others by putting the first information on the table for consideration."[88]

The Bandwagon Effect

"The tendency people have to adopt a certain behavior, style, or attitude simply because everyone else is doing it."[89]

Outcome Bias

"The tendency to evaluate a decision on the basis of its outcome rather than on what factors led to the decision. This form of biased thinking occurs more often with negative events. When decisions lead to poor outcomes, people assign more blame and harsher punishment to the decision maker than if their decision had led to a positive outcome, even if the decision was well thought-out or the probability of success was due to chance."[90]

The Halo Effect

"…generalization from the perception of one outstanding personality trait to an overly favorable evaluation of the whole personality."[91]

Recency Bias

"The tendency to think that trends and patterns we observe in the recent past will continue in the future."[92]

Prejudice may be defined as "an irrational attitude of hostility directed against an individual, a group, a race, or their supposed characteristics."[93]

As American educator Kendra Cherry noted,

Prejudice can have a strong influence on how people behave and interact with others, particularly with those who are different from them, even unconsciously or without the person realizing they are under the influence of their internalized prejudices.[94]

Righteous insistence might be the remnant of a primitive biological need to compete with our peers for survival. We may be driven by the motive (consciously, or perhaps otherwise) to demonstrate the superiority of our knowledge and the magnificence of our intellectual characteristics as we compete for living space, the admiration of others, and sexual dominance.

It might be better to acknowledge that complete certainty in our beliefs about the world (and the people in it) is unwarranted.

Chapter 4
Human Nature and Self-Awareness

Understanding People

This chapter describes what psychologists and philosophers have learned about how perception and comprehension operate.

Perceiving and understanding the world involves a very complex set of dynamic processes.[95] Cognitive psychologists and neuropsychologists have described these functions quite well; this is very fortunate because awareness and comprehension of how we perceive and think enables us to manage our beliefs, feelings and behavior.

Our knowledge and feelings produce our motives and actions, but we can't regulate our mental functions very well if we don't understand how they operate.

We learn to understand ourselves better and manage ourselves more effectively by a) examining our experiences of knowing, feeling, and behaving (applying *mindfulness*, see the section on this subject below) and b) observing, evaluating, and improving our habits of thinking.

> By tracking our mental processes and noticing our cognitive habits through introspection we can learn how our thoughts, motives, and actions operate as a system. We can gain insights into our actions and our reactions which we can apply to improve our productivity, our success, and our satisfaction.

The following section emphasizes the importance of distinguishing our linguistic ideas (concepts) about things (physical objects or experiences) from the things themselves.

Ontology – Understanding the Structure of Reality

"Reality" (existence or being) is an abstract linguistic construct. We don't perceive it as a discrete object – it's far too big (and much too small!) for our senses to grasp. However, most of us agree that some things are real, and we can describe different classes of real things.

Developing deeply coherent sets of ideas about complex processes requires that we comprehend an essential difference between abstract ideas (concepts) and other types of things. This demands that we adopt a philosophical perspective on the kinds of things that we understand and discuss.

Ontology is the study of "the nature of being or the kinds of things that have existence."[96] Ontological theories describe which basic *metaphysical substances* we can identify. These are supposed to represent the lowest common denominators of reality, the fundamental components of existence.

Some theories postulate that only one substance is real, but they differ on what that might be: *materialism* is the idea that only physical things exist, while *idealism* specifies that physical objects are illusory and only non-material things are real.

Dualism is the metaphysical theory that both material and non-material things exist.

In theory, physical objects are different types of things from our conscious experiences, but in practice, they may be conflated. For example, I've noticed that people sometimes overlook the basic distinction between *minds* and *brains*, which consist of different substances. The former refers to people's (non-material) experiences, while the latter is a collection of nerve cells. Our brains don't contain our thoughts or ideas, and our minds are not in our heads.

> Concepts that don't refer to observable physical objects or observable events refer to abstract things.

A *pluralistic* ontology specifies more than two metaphysical categories. To account for everything that *seems* real to people, Popper described three types of substances with which human beings engage (Figure 1).[97]

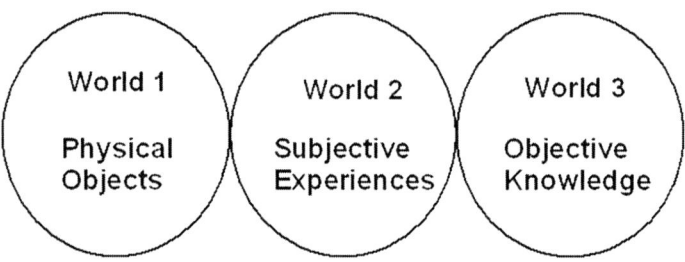

Figure 1. Popper's ontology: Three human realities.

World 1 encompasses physical reality, the world of matter and measurement. World 2 describes subjective experiences (consciousness), and World 3 is the realm of public information (ideas), the socially constructed (abstract linguistic) concepts that humans have generated throughout history.

What we *think* is a subjective experience; what we *say* is physical sound waves, and what we *designate* is an abstract bit of objective knowledge. Popper took great care to emphasize the importance of distinguishing subjective beliefs (World 2) from objective meanings (World 3):

It is the objective thought content of a conjecture or theory on which the scientist's subjective thought processes work. They are at work to improve the objective thought contents by way of criticism.[98]

If we fail to distinguish these two types of things, we can't differentiate subjective personal meanings (thoughts and points of view) from objective public ideas.

Understanding things refers to comprehending the language that refers to them (World 3). The only way to tell whether our ideas are similar to someone else's is to compare how closely their meanings match ours.

Consciousness (World 2) is the link between sensations and ideas; it mediates the relationships between physical materials and subjective meanings. As American poet Henry Wadsworth Longfellow wrote, "All things are symbols: the external shows of Nature have their image in the mind."[99]

Physicality

Physics

Some physicists have provided marvelous insights into the composition of physical things; however, the deeper they've looked the thinner the physical materials have become. They've figured out that solid objects contain mostly empty space, atoms aren't solid particles, and subatomic particles seem to consist of (unobservable) bits of energy (*superstrings*).

Beyond that, 95% of the physical universe is made up of (unobservable) dark energy and dark matter, which have been hypothesized to exist to account for some apparent (gravitational) effects on observable (distant) astronomical objects.[100]

However, some physicists have suggested that new definitions of spacetime itself might be more cogent than any historical model has portrayed; the long-favored "Standard Cosmological Model" (the "Big Bang" theory) is being assailed by new discoveries.[101]

Current theories about the nature of *space* postulate that three-dimensional space exists as a projection of ten spatial dimensions.[102] Furthermore, some theorists believe that an infinite number of universes (a multiverse) exist. I find the latter notion amusing; how could that issue matter to me? Even a dynamic three-dimensional universe (containing three types of metaphysical substances) is too much for anybody to understand very well – I don't think that we have any business in other hypothetical ones!

Although theoretical physics is irrelevant to most of us, we need to deal with the physical world around us. Making sense of physical events and processes is important to everyone. We want to comprehend what we observe, and we need to manipulate many physical objects every day.

Fortunately, ideas about physical things are susceptible to the use of operational methods.[103] If we pay close attention to what's going on around us, like checking the weather forecast and a traffic app to determine how we ought to travel around the city on a given day, then we can optimize the chances that we'll succeed in achieving our goals.

Sensing and Perceiving

Our biological tissues mediate our interactions with the world. Sensation is a biological function that produces conscious experiences (*percepts*).

It should be noted that *we can't actually sense the entirety of any physical object*; we can only sense extremely small bits of things. Our eyes sense *reflected light* – but only a narrow range of wavelengths. Our eardrums detect *sound waves* – also within particular limits. Nerves in the skin sense tactile *pressure* (touch), and we can only taste or smell particular *molecules*. Those are the physical things that we actually sense.

Neuropsychological research on perception indicates that our sense organs relay sets of neural signals to our brains; those signals then activate historical patterns of neural activity which correspond to *language that we've previously learned to describe those particular patterns* (I see a book; I hear music). This process is called *analysis by synthesis*.[104]

Consciousness

Our conscious experiences are the (metaphorical) outer layers of our individual minds. Our historical ones (feelings, thoughts, beliefs, recollections, etc.) somehow remain beneath that surface; they take turns rising to awareness and then subsiding.[105] Our minds continually recreate a vast but limited repertoire of thoughts and feelings, and we undergo many of these experiences again and again for most of our lives.

Our experiences drive us to act in particular ways. Most of the time, our historical understandings take us to where we've already been, but we expand that repertoire (broaden our experience) by exploring novel ideas and unfamiliar practices.

We can decide to seek new environments, meet new mentors, and experience unfamiliar events. We might stumble upon these things, but we learn more effectively when we do it on purpose.

> We may learn incidentally without any particular intention to do so, and we may learn intentionally if we appreciate the value of education enough to remain alert for opportunities to apply self-reflection and self-correction.

Chapters 5, 6 and 7 describe how lifelong learning is related to developing practical wisdom.

For millennia, some people have studied their experiences and taught others to examine their own cognitive and affective processes through meditative techniques. Experienced mentors guide meditators in learning to manage the spontaneous thoughts and desires that continually drive people to behave according to habitual patterns.

Understanding Human Nature

If I were to ask you what it's like to be human, you could tell me what you think and feel about your subjective experiences. If I ask what humans have in common, you'd have to look beyond your own point of view.

Humanity is the nature of human beings. Understanding what it's like to be human is far beyond understanding what *you* think and feel; it's about recognizing how our common thinking and feeling processes operate.

Acknowledging our commonalities is a useful exercise; it facilitates understanding and cooperation. We each identify with our own bodies and our own experiences, but the habit of emphasizing our differences from others while deemphasizing our commonalities may prevent us from understanding each other very well.

Moral values (including solidarity and kindness) are much more difficult to apply if we focus on our differences rather than accentuate our commonalities.

Many of us have had difficulty in dealing effectively with some of our emotions (such as anger, frustration, or sadness). We may believe that these are undesirable experiences. We might hide these emotions from our own consciousness because we don't want to experience them.

Repression has been defined as the tendency to inhibit – consciously or unconsciously – the experience and expression of negative emotions or unpleasant cognitions in order to prevent one's positive self-image from being threatened.[106]

For example, I might be afraid about what might happen when engaged in a serious argument with a friend but repress the fear by becoming angry, overshadowing the fear with a different emotion.

We learn to recognize and accept our fears by examining and managing our anger mechanisms,[107] a process that results in diminishing both anger and fear.[108]

Humans are emotional beings; repressing or denying one's feelings is, in effect, repressing or denying one's humanity. We might want to avoid experiencing fear, hate, shame, disgust, anger, hatred, or grief; when we feel those emotions, we might feel bad *about* feeling bad, which is even worse. We'd consciously bypass these feelings if we could, but we can't dispose of our emotions, which are an integral part of our humanity. The best we can do is manage our reactions to our feelings.

We can observe what we tend to think when we're upset, and what we tend to do. We can notice when our thoughts compel our actions, and we can evaluate the consequences of our compulsions. If we accept our human reactions, then we can learn to react to our emotions without rejecting or resisting them,[109] and we can avoid lashing out at other people when we get upset.

> Fulfillment is facilitated by understanding oneself clearly and communicating authentically. One might think that it's better to appear to be immune to the emotions that affect us deeply, but denying our human nature prevents us from coping with it very effectively.

Characterization

It's common to describe people. We can measure someone's height or weight, count their teeth, and x-ray their bones. There are many standard measures which tell us about people's bodies.

Behaviors are observable, and we can tally the frequencies with which they're produced, thus describing the overt habits and tendencies that people display. Psychologists and psychiatrists use standardized measures of people's behavior to describe *personality types* and to determine people's mental fitness.

We may tend to describe each other, and we may also assess ourselves. It's quite common to use adjectives (labels: derogatory or laudatory, such as *mean* or *generous*) based on subjective opinions to describe someone's *character*.

As a child I learned to classify and characterize people, and I mistakenly thought that my beliefs about them were true. Eventually, I realized that people are much more complex than any label can describe.

In a competitive conversational context (where people work to demonstrate that they're correct about something and that someone else is mistaken), one might use defamatory labels to avoid losing an argument (the *ad hominem* fallacy).

It's quite easy to disparage people by applying subjective opinions without any objective justification (see Chapter 6 on Judging People). Even if a derogatory opinion is very well justified by someone's terrible habits, personalities can't be described coherently by adjectival labels.

Disparaging people with labels is a common method of manifesting one's antagonism or declaring one's (supposed) superiority. Although this practice may be considered abusive and immoral, that doesn't prevent anyone from applying it, even when the justifications for such appraisals are the products of personal prejudices.

As the black/white fallacy indicates, it's always incorrect to believe that such labels are true. Nobody is simply or completely wise, stupid, good, bad, kind, mean, beautiful, or ugly.

Applying Objectivity in Practice

In theory, wisdom is a function of coherence and morality. In practice, it's a matter of applying those ideals to what we say and do, using reliable evidence and clear reasoning to justify our beliefs and actions.

The world of objective knowledge includes more abstract meanings than anyone can learn in a lifetime, and innovative ideas continue to pour in. It's up to each of us to seek out useful information, and to evaluate carefully what we hear and read, so that we may first distinguish and then apply the best ideas that we can find to produce benefits for ourselves and others.

We should keep in mind that deeply coherent thinking doesn't produce the absolute truth about the world. Objects in the (ten dimensional?) physical universe (constructed from superstrings?) are too complex for any human language to describe with complete accuracy.

We can build machines to measure what we can't sense directly, and we can perceive what the machines indicate, but there aren't enough types of machines to measure everything, and we can only *infer* what the measurements reflect. We don't know the *true nature* of *anything* because we only understand linguistic meanings.

Objectivity is a social phenomenon – we apply language to justify our assertions so that other people can understand and evaluate our reasoning. Our thoughts are subjective, but we can articulate and evaluate them through objective (linguistic) methods.

We might sometimes face complex questions about what we ought to do in problematic situations. To apply critical thinking and moral discernment in such circumstances, it may be useful to compare our subjective beliefs and opinions to other people's ideas before deciding which actions are optimal.

> Consideration of what works effectively in practice requires that we apply objective knowledge and ideal values to problem-solving and decision-making. The processes involved in critical thinking (analysis, explanation, and metacognition) and moral discernment (applying ethical discourses) are the means for making value-based objective decisions about what should be done and how to do it.

Types of Intelligence

The ways that people apply language is considered evidence for determining levels of cognitive skill ("intelligence"), but those processes don't represent the entire spectrum of human abilities.

To deepen and broaden our understanding of human nature, we can explore a more global view by recognizing different perspectives on our capabilities. Near the end of the twentieth century psychologists applied this process to transform the idea of human intelligence.

Educational psychologist Robert Sternberg posited a theory of intelligence that focuses on how people learn, describing three categories of intellectual skills. *Knowledge acquisition* refers to learning new information, while *performance* components include inferential (*inductive*) reasoning, "to make sense of the present and predict the future."[110] Finally, *self-regulative meta-components* of intelligence "are used to plan, monitor and evaluate… problem-solving."[111]

Cognitive psychologist Howard Gardner urged scholars to consider other human abilities (aside from linguistic and logical-mathematical skills) that contribute to success in life. He added eight other "intelligences" to describe our various abilities (Table 3).[112]

Intelligence Type	**Skills**
Linguistic	Use of language
Logical-mathematical	Calculation, quantification, and logic
Existential	Insight into human nature
Interpersonal	Work well with others
Bodily-kinesthetic	Movement and timing
Naturalist	Sensitive to events in the natural environment
Musical	Discerning sounds and musical notes
Intrapersonal	Understanding oneself
Spatial	Three-dimensional mental imagery

Table 3. Nine types of human intelligence.

This scheme expands our perspectives on human abilities.

In 1990, psychologists Peter Salovey and John D. Mayer developed the idea of *emotional intelligence*.[113] According to skillsyouneed.com,

People with higher emotional intelligence find it easier to form and maintain interpersonal relationships and to "fit in" to group situations. People with higher emotional intelligence are also better at understanding their own psychological state, which can include managing stress effectively and being less likely to suffer from depression.[114]

Our attitudes toward self-development determine what we might learn. If we intend to increase our skills, we can apply ourselves to developing the self-regulatory capabilities that are crucial to developing all forms of intelligence.

Problem-Solving

An *algorithm* is a predefined process, a series of steps that are applied to solve relatively simple problems. For example, the instructions for boiling an egg or installing a furnace are algorithmic. However, more complex problems (such as how to design a bridge, or how to get from New York to Detroit most quickly in a heavy snowstorm) aren't amenable to being resolved by simple rules.

Applying *heuristics* refers to figuring out how to resolve complex problems without an algorithm, using broad guidelines combined with analytical and creative skills to produce novel approaches and solutions.

Many theorists have described the heuristic guidelines for resolving complex problems.[115] They describe an iterative process that is repeated until satisfactory resolutions are implemented (Table 4).

Heuristic Problem-Solving

1. Identify the problem and its context

Document all relevant details, for example, Where and under what circumstances is the problematic situation occurring? Who are the people who are affected and how are they affected? What are the desired results and how are they supposed to be achieved? Who's involved in working to resolve the situation and what tools are available to support the resolution process?

---

2. Analyze the problem and context (causation and consequences)

Identify the processes involved in the situation. Gather relevant information from the stakeholders to determine where the processes might be changed or improved. Decide what other information is required to define and analyze the problem in its entirety.

3. Consider alternative solutions

Define (or redefine) future processes and methods to produce the desired results. Consider various ways to address each issue to be addressed, in terms of benefits, efforts required, and potential costs.

4. Identify the best solution

Decide which actions are likely to produce optimal results. Create benchmarks to determine the degree of success after implementation.

5. Implement the best solution

Inform all stakeholders of changes to the processes; solicit and consider their suggestions and apply them where appropriate.

6. Evaluate results of implementation

Monitor results. Review benchmarks and develop ideas for future improvements. Review the problem-solving process to learn from the experience. If benchmarks aren't met, repeat the entire process.

Table 4. Heuristics.

Self-Awareness

As Kendra Cherry points out, "Self-awareness involves being aware of different aspects of the self, including traits, behaviors, and feelings."[116]

Many self-styled experts have claimed to understand the truth about the human mind. Some truth seekers have elevated that idea above almost everything else, enabling some of the truth mongers to be highly successful in attracting believers and gaining wealth.

> Wisdom doesn't demand understanding the Truth of the Universe or the Truth of the Self. Instead, it requires distinguishing what we can describe very clearly from what we can't understand very well.

Introspection, the examination of our subjective experiences, is the beginning of self-awareness, and many ways to ponder human consciousness have been developed.

Israeli educator Yuval Noah Harari concluded his thoughtful and informative treatise *21 Lessons for the 21st Century*[117] with a chapter on meditation. He noted that his personal journey (which led him to remarkable academic and literary success) includes an essential focus on that practice. I share his appreciation for meditation and its roots, which include the philosophy developed by Siddhartha Gautama (known as Buddha) twenty-five hundred years ago.

Some practitioners consider Buddhism a religion, although no deity is involved in its theories or practices.

Gautama suggested that human life entails suffering, which results from ignorance about our psychological cravings. He noted that this pain is diminished through understanding and embracing our human foibles. With practice, we can experience less suffering (and more joy!) by becoming less attached to our hopes and wishes (unfulfilled desires). Chapter 6 contains a section on this subject (Diminishing Suffering).

The value of *moderation* may be especially important when it comes to developing wisdom and being fulfilled. One of the practical recommendations of Buddhist philosophy, the *Middle Way*,[118] asserts that we should avoid extreme ideas and actions. This resembles Aristotle's description of the *Golden Mean*,[119] which also recommends taking the middle course between deficiency and excess.

Some people rely very heavily on thinking, discounting the relevance of feelings and emotions when deciding what to do. Others are very emotional and intuitive, with little desire to consider reasons or evidence at great length when making decisions. It may be important to navigate between these extremes, applying our metacognitive resources to considering objective ideas, and managing our desires through metamotivation, when deciding what to do and how to do it.

Interdependency is the idea that related processes affect each other by operating together. Thinking and feeling (cognition and affect) are two poles of human consciousness; together, they determine our attitudes and tendencies. What we think influences what we feel, and what we feel influences what we think. In theory, these two sets of processes are distinct from each other, but in practice, they're functionally intertwined.

Mindfulness (Presence of Mind)

Mindfulness (being present or *being in the moment*) refers to the possibility of detachment from our inferences and our stories about what's happened, what might have happened, or what might happen. It means attending to our experiences as they occur, one after another.

Meditation, which is designed to focus on one's experiences from moment to moment, is a useful tool for developing mindfulness. However, mindfulness isn't simply a matter of meditating or relaxing; it's an educational objective that has been promoted by many sages as essential to spirituality and self-fulfillment.

According to Buddhist philosophy, the more mindful we become the more effectively we can attend to eight aspects of human life related to self-development and applying practical wisdom (described in Chapter 6).

Humanism

Individual responsibility is an important aspect of practical wisdom. Humanism requires that we each decide how to behave, rather than following the directions of religious or political authorities.

For millennia, the dominant philosophy in the civilized world was theism, the notion that a Divine Being rules the cosmos. People who didn't subscribe to the idea that God made the rules for humankind were labeled heretical; many were excommunicated, punished, and/or executed for their transgressions.

Francis Bacon produced the foundation of scientific analysis in 1620,[120] and a novel perspective began to erode the theistic approach. As described by newworldencyclopedia.org,

Humanism is an attitude of thought which gives primary importance to human beings…Enlightenment humanism…produced atheism, Marxism, as well as secular humanism. Secular humanism, which denies God and attributes the universe entirely to material forces, today has replaced religion for many people.[121]

While humanism elevates the value of individual responsibility, it raises some important questions. For example, should we consider human life itself as the highest of all values? If not, how then would one decide what's more important? How does one measure the value of sacrificing people's lives to produce something that's more important? When is euthanasia (or suicide) an acceptable moral alternative to living with chronic pain? Are we responsible for the well-being of animals, and (if so) how can we balance human needs with a commitment to treat animals as sentient beings?

Professional ethicists parse these questions into operational principles for dealing with medical, legal, and political questions.

Chapter 5
Educating for Wisdom

Developing Wisdom

Practical wisdom is the process of applying critical analysis and moral values (in context) to decide what people should or shouldn't do.

Higher-order thinking involves resolving cognitive puzzles and conflicts. Of course, it's simpler and easier to avoid thinking deeply.

Truth adherents don't need to provide coherent justifications for their ideas. If confronted with a reasonable argument contrary to their views, True Believers can bluster, resort to fallacious reasoning, change the subject, or withdraw from the conversation.

I've met many highly educated and very clever people who hold strong opinions on many subjects and think that their beliefs reflect the absolute truths about unobservable realities. It's practically inconceivable to them that they might be mistaken about anything important, so they don't inquire deeply into other perspectives.

> If we don't embrace fallibilism as the most reasonable approach to human understanding, we might project the absurd belief that we're immune to being mistaken.

People who develop deep wisdom do so because they want to. If we have ambitions to achieve and difficult issues to manage, then resolving complex issues becomes a way of life.

Some people believe that they lack the capacity to develop strong cognitive powers. Being right about the limits of one's capabilities (a self-fulfilling prophecy) is very easy to do, and it's also self-defeating. On the other hand, it's impossible to predict what healthy adults might learn if we work at it.

Developing deeply coherent sets of ideas about complex subjects such as human functionality and moral reasoning isn't a measurable goal or a short-term occupation. Cognitive development requires an ongoing commitment to self-regulation.

In the past fifty years science, medicine, and engineering have produced profound changes in human civilization, which have had severe effects on our planet's ecosystem. Industrial conglomerates, transportation and aerospace technology, social media, and artificial intelligence have changed the world in ways that nobody could have anticipated a century ago.

Climate change, pollution, and social unrest (including international conflicts and terrorism) represent dire threats to humanity. We don't know what the next decades will bring, but it seems obvious that resolving these issues would require global cooperation on a scale that hasn't yet been achieved.

Complexity

Higher-order thinking is a matter of focusing on complexity.

Consider the course of education from early childhood. We begin to develop our senses while in the womb; after birth, we begin to notice physical objects (including our bodies), and we learn to sort external stimuli and our reactions to them into categories (objects, people, comfort, discomfort, etc.). This process becomes increasingly complicated as we develop abstract ideas.

Simple concepts (linguistic *categories*) refer to observable physical objects or actions (such as ball, knife, kick, laugh…). These basic ideas refer to observable things that are amenable to operational measures.

American educational psychologist Kurt Fischer and his associates described how those ideas are combined to form more complex ones, which can't be observed or measured directly.[122] He noted that "second level" abstractions denote *sets* (combinations) of the simplest concepts.

For example, the idea *forest* refers to many different observable things (trees of course, but other things as well). This means that we can't measure it directly. However, we can assess the condition of the soil in various sectors, and we can describe the diverse types of local plants and animals to inform us about the condition of a particular forest.

Second-level abstractions are combined into even more complex (third level) ideas (*systems*). For example, *ecology* refers to a system that includes cities, bodies of water, plants, animals, and people in a specific area.

The fourth level of abstraction (a *system of systems*) combines systems into hypercomplex constructs. For example, *science* refers to all the systems associated with that term: biology, astronomy, etc.

> To clarify their meanings, we analyze complex abstract ideas by breaking them down into their basic (operational) components. Any cogent analysis of third or fourth level concepts (systems or systems of systems) requires expanding their descriptions into second level concepts, and then into simple ones.

We can examine, alter, and recombine our abstract ideas until our linguistic perspectives are well supported by clear evidence: observable facts (relevant and reliable data).

Of course, most of us have more useful things to do than spend our time analyzing systems of systems. However, we may be inclined to resolve the cognitive challenges that relate to achieving our most important goals.

Developing Critical Discourses

American philosopher and educator Matthew Lipman championed educational applications of research into higher-order thinking.

If we want to foster and strengthen critical thinking in the schools and colleges, we...need a clear conception of what critical thinking can be. Therefore, it will be very useful to know its defining features, its characteristic outcomes, and the underlying conditions that make it possible.[123]

Lipman also acknowledged that promoting metacognition is vital in education.

One of the most important advantages of converting the classroom into a community of inquiry is that the members of the community begin looking for and correcting each other's methods and procedures. Consequently, insofar as each participant is able to internalize the methodology of the community as a whole, each is able to become self-correcting in his or her own thinking.[124]

Educators distinguish simple (*well-defined* or *well-structured*) problems, which are solved by applying a predefined series of steps (an *algorithm)*, from *ill-defined* or *ill-structured* problems for which algorithms aren't available. Higher-order thinking applies heuristic methods to analyze and resolve complex ill-structured problems.

Psychologist Diane Halpern decried the failure of "college students and the American public in general"[125] to use critical cognition to justify their beliefs. She wrote,

Higher-order skills are relatively complex, require judgment, analysis, and synthesis, and are not applied in a rote or mechanical manner. The goal of instruction designed to help students become better thinkers is transferability to real-life, out-of-the-classroom situations.[126]

American educators Richard Paul and Linda Elder bemoaned the failure of social institutions to emphasize the value of critical thinking skills, writing, "Great power is wielded around the world by little minds."[127] They emphasized that reconciling conflicting points of view requires flexibility and breadth of vision. They noted that effective and rational decision-makers are aware of, and are able to re-evaluate, their "most fundamental goals, purposes, and needs."

Paul and Elder described the purposes involved in thinking critically, including the achievement of clarity, significance, consistency, and justifiability.

According to these authors, deep thinkers describe situations and alternative courses of action as precisely as they can, and they consider the consequences and the implications of each alternative. They actively seek relevant information, which they analyze and interpret carefully, evaluating each option in the light of circumstances, and adopting an appropriate strategy that addresses all of the above. Finally, competent decision-makers monitor and evaluate the consequences of their actions and are ready to modify their analyses and change their strategies as more information becomes available.

American educational psychologist Robert Sternberg argued that schools should prepare students for life by teaching cognitive skills.[128] He noted that to succeed in higher learning students must be motivated to think carefully and learn to combine workable learning strategies with appropriate mental representations of things and processes in the world.

People who adopt these practices are more likely to succeed in their academic and non-academic endeavors than those who don't.

American philosopher Nel Noddings suggested that the most basic moral issue is caring for others. This leaves us with the constant problem of balancing people's interests in every social endeavor, which sometimes calls for careful consideration of ethical issues.

Noddings endorsed Aristotle's idea that "The virtues identified in the very best citizens"[129] should be taught to children as a matter of course as they mature because "Recognition of the pluralism of values...suggests the need for careful analysis of the virtues."[130]

> Higher-order cognitive development is intentionally produced by applying critical analysis and explanation *in context* to decide a) which ideas are more sensible than others and b) which actions or activities produce more benefits and less harm. We increase our chances of achieving our most ambitious goals by developing these distinctions.

Early Childhood Education

We begin to learn language by grasping the simplest ideas. We eventually progress to higher levels of linguistic sophistication.

In early life, we each acquired a set of fundamental viewpoints (*presumptive beliefs*) from the people around us. We absorbed ideas as quickly as they were explained to us, and we believed what we were told because *that's what there was for us to learn*.

No matter how open-minded caregivers might be, they can only teach what they understand.

Young children can't think very well for themselves because they have little information and haven't yet figured out how to sort what they hear according to coherency. They use what they know as well as they can, and they're hungry to learn more.

When children begin to think for themselves, they may be encouraged to do so, or they might be discouraged from believing anything that contradicts what they're being taught. In strongly authoritarian environments, *skepticism* is forbidden, *faith* is required, and *obedience* is also mandatory.

Eventually, some of us figured out that we were fed beliefs that weren't true. Others continue to believe as adults that the fundamental presumptions they learned as children are absolutely correct and must forever remain so.

Italian philosopher Antonio Gramsci noted how knowledge is transmitted in an authoritarian society. His description of *cultural hegemony* refers to the maintenance of strict ideological standards. As sociologist Nicki Lisa Cole explained,

Cultural hegemony refers to domination or rule maintained through ideological or cultural means. It is usually achieved through *social institutions, which allow those in power to strongly influence the values, norms, ideas, expectations, worldview, and behavior of the rest of society.*

Cultural hegemony functions by framing the worldview of the ruling class, and the social and economic structures that embody it, as just, legitimate, and designed for the benefit of all, even though these structures may only benefit the ruling class. This kind of power is distinct from rule by force, as in a military dictatorship, because it allows the ruling class to exercise authority using the "peaceful" means of ideology and culture.[131]

In the last half of the 20th century, French philosopher Michel Foucault produced persuasive arguments to support the view that power and knowledge aren't distinct from each other, but are inextricably linked in practice. As he wrote, "The exercise of power perpetually creates knowledge and, conversely, knowledge constantly induces effects of power."[132]

The educational philosophy called *critical pedagogy* calls attention to the authoritative presumptions that underlie teacher's perspectives.[133] Danish educator Finn Mogensen recommended that teachers should acknowledge the significance of presumptive beliefs, writing:

This means, among other things, recognizing that what exists is always encapsulated in cultural and historical contexts. Critical reflections should reach an understanding of how these contexts have influenced the thinker. From this basis, critical thinking should develop the ability to imagine alternatives and propose possible modes of action. Critical thinking is visionary thinking.[134]

As American educator Cynthia Luna Scott noted,

Since the emergence of a global movement that calls for a new model of learning for the twenty-first century, it has been argued that formal education must be transformed to enable new forms of learning that are needed to tackle complex global challenges. Literature on this topic offers compelling arguments for transforming pedagogy to better support acquisition of twenty-first century skills.[135]

Learning Environments

Learning environments include many educational materials that are utilized in a variety of methods. Some materials and methods are suitable for young learners, others for more advanced inquirers.

When I went to grade school in the 1950s, there was a lot of talking, writing, and a bit of other action. The teacher read to us, and we read to the teacher. The teacher asked simple questions, and we answered them correctly or incorrectly. We did exercises and quizzes at our desks.

Things have changed somewhat. The old model was *teacher-centered*, with the focus on what the teacher said or did. We were there to learn what we were told to learn and do what we were told to do. Nowadays, it's understood that more active student *engagement* facilitates learning better than the teacher-centered approach.

Teaching is teacher-centered, but *learning is student-centered*. The more that learners engage with their subjects, the better they learn; the more they learn, the better they can engage.

Since people have diverse learning styles, educational tools are more suited to some learners than others. The most effective learning environments provide various methods for learning the same lessons.[136]

Figure 2 presents four levels of student engagement, which are associated with particular educational techniques and cognitive practices (skills or *competencies*).

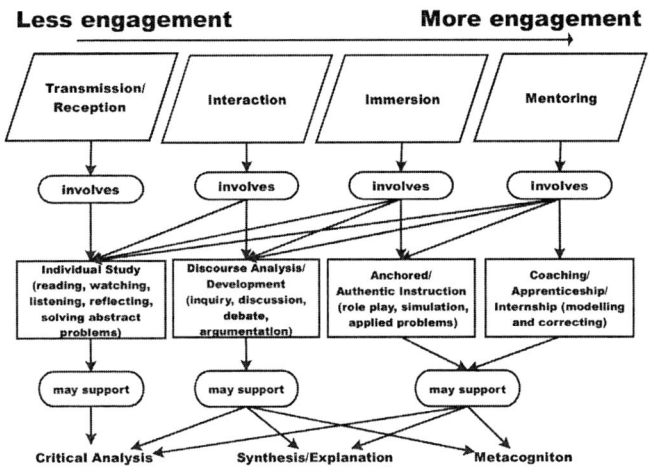

Figure 2. Levels of engagement (top row), associated methods (rectangles), and cognitive skills (bottom row).

The least engaging methods include watching and listening (transmission and reception); students are accountable for paying attention to lectures and presentations and for retaining information about what they heard or saw. Solving math problems and doing individual exercises is slightly more engaging but doesn't involve interacting with other minds. These methods support the possibility of developing critical analysis, but they offer little instructional support for doing so.

Interactive discussions represent a higher level of engagement with a subject. Asking questions and debating alternative perspectives enable teachers and students to analyze each other's ideas and figure things out together. This allows the possibility for instructors to model critical inquiry by referring to evidence, describing reasoning, and demonstrating how they monitor, evaluate, and correct their own opinions. Students get to practice critical thinking techniques, including analysis, explanation, and self-correction.

Immersive methods provide a range of activities to be performed, including those that relate to life outside of classrooms. *Anchored* techniques relate to educational activities rather than theoretical discussions; students may plant gardens, build robots, or participate in role-playing games and computer simulations. Field trips and class projects take students into unfamiliar environments and provide opportunities for a much deeper investigation of the world than is possible in classrooms. Virtual reality provides opportunities for access to artificial environments that can be designed for any educational purpose.

> The most engaging and intensive educational method is *mentoring*, a long-term association with an experienced educator. Students can learn what their mentors understand, and mentors guide students in learning how to figure things out for themselves.

Skilled instructors ask questions and provide explanations that enable learners to comprehend previously unconsidered ideas, meanings, and practices. Russian psychologist Lev Vygotsky described how parents and teachers lead children from simple perspectives to more complex ones by introducing topics that extend their awareness just beyond their current thinking.[137] This practice (*cognitive scaffolding*) provides educational steps to more complex ideas and activities.

Adult Learning

American educator Malcolm Knowles described self-directed adult learners as those who have developed "a deep psychological need to be perceived by others, and treated by others, as capable of taking responsibility for [themselves]."[138]

He observed that adults who participate in educational practices are often highly motivated to do so. They're usually prepared to work hard to achieve their learning objectives and to support others in doing the same. As Knowles wrote, "the more potent motivators are internal – self-esteem, recognition, better quality of life, greater self-confidence, self-actualization and the like."[139]

As young children, we understood very well that we needed to learn. We realized that there was a great deal that we didn't know and that it was important to keep educating ourselves for years to come.

After a couple of decades (more or less), we narrowed our future prospects and decided what we wanted to learn. We may have also decided the limits of our abilities.

Education programs are no longer directed exclusively at children or young adults. Some of us have decided to educate ourselves throughout our lifetimes; personal fulfillment may be incrcased by applying this commitment in action.

Knowles depicted education as a lifelong process of active inquiry and goal-striving. He described the core methodology of adult learning as the analysis of one's experiences, noting that the most competent learners continually anticipate what's to come, are cooperative, creative, self-directed, efficient, altruistic, tolerant, rational, and have broad interests. In a self-directed process, mature learners define their educational needs and interests, plan their learning, organize the process (engaging in *learning contracts* with their instructors), and evaluate their results. Educational practices are performance-centered, problem-centered, and life-centered. Instructors and learners are joint inquirers in a spirit of friendly, informal, supportive, and democratic mutuality.[140]

> If the benefits of deep thinking and lifelong learning are communicated to students in elementary and secondary schools, adults will be better equipped to learn how to achieve their most ambitious endeavors.

Transformative Learning

Brittannica.com recounts French psychologist Jean Piaget's description of how children modify their beliefs when confronted with evidence that their ideas are mistaken.

Piaget conceived *equilibration* [maintaining stable sets of interrelated beliefs in a cognitive equilibrium] as an ongoing process which refines and transforms mental structures, constituting the basis of cognitive development…Equilibration explains an individual's motivation for development. Individuals naturally seek equilibrium because disequilibrium, which is *a mismatch between one's way of thinking and one's environment, is inherently dissatisfying. When individuals encounter new discrepant information, they enter into a state of disequilibrium*. In order to return to a state of equilibrium, individuals can ignore the information or attempt to manage it.[141]

Transformative learning occurs when one realizes that one's past perspective on something has been erroneous and the prior knowledge is superseded by a more coherent and more comprehensive perspective.

Metacognitive self-regulation (*unlearning* and relearning) is applied when we see the benefit of exchanging one perspective for another that's clearly more cogent.[142]

Children are especially quick to realign their conceptual frameworks to deal with novel information. Most adults seem to experience such transformations less often (some of us, perhaps, hardly ever).

Transformative learning is effective not only for individuals but also at the level of social standards. For example, scientists who work to resolve complex problems at the forefront of research have learned to think in established patterns (hegemonies); these theories define which discourses are justifiable within a particular area of study. Thomas Kuhn called these hegemonies in the science community *scientific paradigms*.[143]

Kuhn pointed out that breakthroughs occurred when innovative theorists disregarded established theories and constructed better ones by *rethinking the authoritative interpretations of evidence that had previously been used* to guide research in their fields of study.

By applying a novel interpretation of available evidence (one that provides more explanatory and predictive power than the previously established theory), a scientist is said to have *broken* the old paradigm and created a new one.

American sociologist Jack Mezirow described the importance of *disorienting dilemmas*, which occur when an unexpected occurrence demonstrates that something that one believes must be false. The event produces a sense of inadequacy, a realization that one's prior interpretations are unjustifiable.[144]

For example, when I was a business professional I thought highly of my success and my cleverness. I believed that I was better educated than most other people, but I had difficulties in communicating well with many of them.

I had no clue how my ideas about myself interfered with my social skills, but I figured it out in a psychology workshop where I was working to develop my self-understanding and my communication skills. At one point, I stated a (strong) opinion, and someone turned to me and asked, "Do you know that you're very arrogant?"

Everyone looked at me closely to get my reaction. I automatically and defensively responded, "No I'm not!"

They all smiled and nodded, and almost as one they said, "Really?"

"See?"

"Now do you get it?"

I'd previously thought that arrogance meant *the act of insisting that an inaccurate claim was true*. I understood at that point that it also refers to *an attitude of superiority*. I realized at that moment that my belief about myself (that my opinions were more informed and more coherent than theirs) was clearly evident to people who understood how arrogance operates.

I've been working to develop humility ever since. Soon afterward (in my first philosophy course!) I learned that even my best ideas shouldn't be considered as absolute truths.

In theory, we can learn to think in different (and better) ways. We can alter our beliefs to improve our lives and increase our satisfaction in ways that we haven't yet imagined.

> In practice, if our convictions prevent us from gaining the satisfaction that we desire, we can reconsider our views and discuss them with others. We can gain fresh insights into how we operate and learn new perspectives. This process facilitates communication, cooperation, and social flourishing.

Complex Dynamic Systems

We can deal with complexity, but to do so, we must tailor our beliefs and practices to account for how things change over time.

The human world is dynamic; things are continually changing – some very rapidly and some so slowly that they seem practically static.

For example, linguistic meanings aren't fixed. The operative meanings of abstract ideas may remain quite stable over time (such as *kindness* or *astronomy*) or change so quickly that no individual can track them (like *technology* or *pollution*).

To understand (in theory) how processes change over time, *mathematical systems theory* (mathematical representations of dynamic system processes) illustrates how simple systems differ from complex ones and how changes may be more or less predictable.

In mathematics, a *line* is a *one-dimensional* set of points. Lines are described by a single variable (*length*).

A *plane* is a two-dimensional space that contains two variables (length and width). A three-dimensional space includes a third level of complexity (depth).

A system is a set of related variables. A *dynamic system* is one where the values of the variables change over time.

We can think of a line that gets longer and/or shorter over time, a plane figure that changes shape, or a three-dimensional solid that may expand or contract to form any number of configurations.

The overall *state* of a system is a list of the values of each variable at a single point in time.

In theory, there's no limit to the number of dimensions that mathematics describes. More dimensions (more variables) provide higher levels of complexity. Highly complex systems comprise many variables.

Changes in some of the variables (effects) are considered to be influenced by variance in some others (causes). Hungarian physicist Péter Érdi pointed out that simple dynamic systems can be described in terms of one cause and one effect, with slight changes to the cause resulting in minor changes to the effect in a predictable manner.[145]

On the other hand, a *complex* dynamic system might comprise the relationships of dozens (or hundreds) of dimensions.

If a system contains only a few dimensions and *if the mathematical functions describing them remain constant* (a *stable* system), then we can make relatively accurate predictions of its future performance.

On the other hand, *if the functions vary rather than remain constant, or if we can't measure all the variables, then prediction is problematic.*

Érdi pointed out that (according to variations in their functionality) highly complex systems may contain circular causality, logical paradoxes, and strange loops, so minor changes to causal influences may produce dramatic effects, and results are unpredictable (*emergent*). For example, our biological functions deteriorate as we age, so we can't predict our health very far into the future.

We can apply the principle of complex system dynamics to the development of linguistic discourses. Fischer's model of cognitive complexity describes how cognition progresses from understanding and expressing simple language (operational concepts) to analyzing and explaining compounded abstractions at increasing levels of complexity.

Linguistic systems are designed to derive meanings from symbols. Each symbol may represent a point in linguistic space. A discourse may involve many variables (potential meanings of various words) to produce a sentence, and thousands of them to tell a story.

As Érdi noted,

The notion of cognitive complexity…has been used as a basis of discussion on the complexity of personal constructions of the real world…The complexity of the world view of a subject can be measured. [For example] a subject with the ability to see people as a mixture of "good" and "bad" characteristics has a higher "cognitive complexity" [than one who sees friends as good people and enemies as bad ones].[146]

Human language has evolved to describe high-level abstractions (such as 'ecosystem' or 'universe'), which incorporate thousands of concepts into one overarching idea.

Transformation for Educators

As a political issue, language operates as a site of struggle among diverse groups who police its usage.

Critical pedagogy describes how our beliefs, motives, and attitudes are embedded in authoritative historical hegemonies. Educators Peter McLaren and Henry Giroux have credited language as the "vehicle for identity, knowledge, and power."

Pedagogically, language provides the self-definitions upon which people act, negotiate various subject positions, and undertake a process of naming and renaming the relations between themselves, others, and the world…As the cultural mask of hegemony, language is being mobilized to police the borders of an ideologically discursive divide that separates dominant from subordinate groups, whites from Blacks, and schools from the imperatives of democratic public life.[147]

Critical pedagogy may be applied to educational practices. For example, *reflective practice* is a program of applying metacognitive self-regulation to facilitate one's professional development.[148]

Stephen Brookfield elucidated his experiences of being a reflective university professor, describing the importance of adapting to the contingencies of teaching and learning situations:

Critically reflective teaching happens when we identify and scrutinize the assumptions that undergird how we work. The most effective way to become aware of these assumptions is to view our practices from different perspectives.[149]

These perspectives comprise various dimensions; some are autobiographical, while others are gained from students, colleagues, and literature.

Brookfield described critical reflection as "anchored in values of justice, fairness, and compassion…critical reflection urges us to create conditions under which each person is respected, valued, and heard."[150]

American educator Kenneth A. Bruffee described the idea of *acculturation* into new cognitive perspectives.[151] Like Brookfield, Bruffee stressed the value of collaboration and emphasized the value of inquiry. He argued that *re-acculturation* (the changing of cultural contexts and integration into new communities of knowledge) should be seen as an essential educational objective.

These examples illustrate how some educators are immersed in a culture of transformation, environments where educators and students intentionally apply metacognition to achieve higher levels of functionality.

Barriers to Transformative Education

There are some difficulties associated with the pedagogical practice of working to support people in altering their meaning perspectives.

One difficulty is psychological: if we're accustomed to relying on hegemonic presumptions, it may be very difficult to learn any ideas that contradict our current knowledge. Cognitive bias interferes with the process.

We identify with our beliefs as parts of us, and suddenly realizing that one of them is less than optimally functional (or perhaps even nonsensical) can be a painful experience, an uncomfortable combination of confusion and shame.

Sophophobia is the fear of learning. As described by author Diane Coutu,

Learning anxiety comes from being afraid to try something new for fear that it will be too difficult, that we will look stupid in the attempt, or that we will have to part from old habits that have worked for us in the past.[152]

When faced with evidence contrary to our ideas, we might retreat to dogmatic certainty, dismissing the facts without considering potential alternative explanations that would undermine our already-understood ideas.

Some of us prefer to avoid educational environments where self-correction might be recommended or required.

Even if learners are sincere about their intentions to restructure their ideas, facing a disorienting dilemma might be so discomfiting that they're compelled to escape a potential learning situation. In contrast, people who are experienced in transformative learning see such situations as opportunities for self-correction.

A second difficulty may involve teachers and administrators who are committed to foundational principles (such as truth) and are suspicious of more recent pedagogical approaches. Encouraging their students to think for themselves may be seen as a threat to their authority, a source of difficulty in managing unruly dissent.

Until education for transformation is fully accepted in the academic mainstream, that approach may be rejected by faculty who are unfamiliar with its bases in contemporary philosophical and psychological theory, or are fearful of its impact on the established order of things.

Chapter 6
Producing Self-Fulfillment

Happiness

The notion of *happiness* is used to refer to experiences of joy or pleasure. It may also be defined as a long-term assessment of one's personal fulfillment (i.e., *life satisfaction*, or *contentment*).

With regard to transient experiences of pleasure, it's possible to develop a habitual tendency towards joyfulness. We can learn to bring joy to life on purpose.[153]

We can create opportunities for enjoying ourselves and for supporting others in doing so.[154] We can intentionally produce circumstances that will bring pleasure to someone or to a group of people.

Fulfilment may also be seen as a highly desirable objective. This ideal is defined by the Cambridge Dictionary as "a feeling of happiness because you are doing what you intended to do in life."[155]

According to the New World Encyclopedia,

Some positive psychologists…have advanced a conception of happiness as "life-satisfaction." In this view, the notion of well-being captures the notion of long-term assessment of happiness, and the subjective experience of happiness is simply conceived as one part of well-being. Life satisfaction is achieved by accomplishing what we deem most important in life.[156]

While we can't measure our experiences objectively, we can subjectively monitor our own well-being at a given moment. We can also assess how fulfilled we've been historically by recalling the frequency with which we've experienced triumph, pleasure, shame, and pain at various times in the past.

In practice, we can evaluate how well today has gone quite easily. It's a bit more difficult to rate a week's worth of living or to evaluate one's satisfaction over the past month or year. Yet, we might recall whether we've been more fulfilled in the past year than we remember being a decade ago.

> If we're not as fulfilled as we'd like to be, we could reflect on how to achieve more satisfaction.

Unfortunately, there's no formula or algorithm for producing success or fulfillment. However, many disciplines have been (or could be) applied as contexts for intentional self-development.

It's no coincidence that such programs usually require us to develop commitments to self-regulation.

For example, the philosophy of Buddhism recommends education and meditation as practices that may be applied to promote mental discipline. Tenzin Gyatso (the Fourteenth Dalai Lama) pointed out that contentment is achieved through training one's mind.

One begins by identifying those factors which lead to happiness and those factors which lead to suffering. Having done this, one then sets about gradually eliminating those factors which lead to suffering and cultivating those which lead to happiness…As long as there is a lack of the inner discipline that brings calmness of mind, external facilities or conditions will never give you the feeling of joy and happiness that you are seeking. On the other hand, if you possess this inner quality, a calmness of mind, a degree of stability within, then even if you lack various external facilities that you would normally consider necessary for happiness, it is still possible to live a happy and joyful life.[157]

Some of our beliefs may produce more suffering than pleasure, and some of our behavioral habits might do more harm than good. Recognizing this aspect of the human condition enables us to identify the "factors" that we want to eliminate or cultivate.

Whatever one's situation or habits might be, well-being may be increased by practicing effective and beneficent habits of action. The more we succeed at that, the more satisfaction we experience and the more fulfilled (and confident) we become.

Possibilities for Self-Development

In 1954, American psychologist Abraham Maslow published his theory of *self-actualization* to describe what he called a *hierarchy of needs*.[158] His original five-tiered framework describes human development as a series of steps that lead toward self-actualization. Maslow added a higher level (transcendence) a quarter-century later to acknowledge that people can advance beyond attachment to our identities.[159]

Table 5 describes these stages from lowest to highest.

Type of Need	Examples
Basic (physiological)	Nutrition, water, warmth, sleep
Safety (security)	Shelter, access to resources
Social (belonging)	Partners, intimacy, love
Esteem	Sense of achievement, confidence
Self-actualization	Self-expression, creativity, morality, contentment
Transcendence	Identification with nature (including human nature)

Table 5. Maslow's hierarchy of needs.

In this scheme, each level is instrumental to the next step. Safety and security depend on the fulfillment of physiological (survival) needs. Love and belonging are facilitated by being secure, and all of those factors contribute to self-esteem and being respected by others.

Self-actualization becomes possible when lower levels are being fulfilled. A self-actualized life is moral, creative, spontaneous, meaningful, and purposeful.

Applying Commitment in Action

To experience the satisfaction we desire, we can approach life as an open possibility for developing our capabilities. If there's something important that we want to make happen, then we may decide to learn how to achieve it.

Self-development is facilitated by acknowledging that we have two distinct views of ourselves and then applying that distinction in action. These are a) our (historical) *identities* – how we understand ourselves to have been, and b) our (ideal) *self-images* – how we'd like to be. The differences between these two representations indicate possibilities for progress.

If we so desire, we may plan specific ways to change our habits.

> When we distinguish how we've been from how we intend to become, we can describe in *operational terms* what we need to learn to do differently to increase our satisfaction. Then we can set our learning objectives and performance goals.

Applying commitment effectively requires that we pay close attention to specifying exactly what we intend to produce. It also requires using operational measures and appropriate timing.

From that perspective, we can make consequential decisions every day about which values we'll manifest on purpose (our commitments), which specific goals we'll achieve, and which actions we'll take to accomplish them.

The SMART method has been developed to indicate how to set clear and attainable goals. It stipulates that our objectives should be *S*pecific (that is *M*easurable), *A*chievable, *R*elevant (to our purposes), and *T*ime-limited.[160]

Timeliness is essential for defining success and failure. If we don't set deadlines for the various goals that we're juggling, we can't plan our actions very effectively. Vague promises without time limits are poor self-motivators; they're inconsistent with the process of applying our commitments effectively in action.

The better we manage our thoughts, feelings, and actions, the better equipped we are to learn to satisfy ourselves and work well with others.

> In theory, we can plan how to produce our desired lifestyles. In practice, we can inquire into what we might do to produce greater fulfillment, decide which goals we intend to achieve, and then figure out how to accomplish them.

People's greatest achievements aren't usually earned easily or quickly. If our goals are very ambitious, we'll need to work hard to learn how to achieve them. We won't always succeed on the first (or second, or third) attempt, but by reviewing each failure we can learn more and more about how to achieve our aims.

Diminishing Suffering

As noted in Chapter 4, Buddhist philosophy includes the understanding that human life necessarily includes emotional suffering.

We're always subject to our feelings (transient states of being).[161] Gautama claimed that acknowledging the transitory nature of our experiences produces the possibility of reducing suffering by recognizing and managing its source: *attachment* (striving for lasting satisfaction in a world of impermanent phenomena). As Tenzin Gyatso explained,

According to Buddhist psychology, most of our troubles are due to our passionate desire for and attachment to things that we misapprehend as enduring entities.[162]

Three centuries later the Greek philosopher Epictetus also recognized that "...freedom is not secured by the fulfilment of people's desires, but by the suppression of desire."[163]

This isn't to say that we shouldn't have attachments – they're included in our human nature. It simply indicates that we can learn to avoid dwelling on them.

Gautama's system includes an educational program for self-development, the Eightfold Path (Table 6).[164]

Wisdom	**Morality**	**Concentration**
Right Understanding	Right Speech	Right Effort
Right Aspiration	Right Action	Right Mindfulness
	Right Livelihood	Right Meditation

Table 6. The Eightfold Path

These disciplines emphasize the values of coherency ("understanding"), motivation ("aspiration"), and morality. They also require the application of psychological self-regulation since "right mindfulness" includes:

Mindfulness of body
Mindfulness of feelings or sensations
Mindfulness of mind or mental processes
Mindfulness of mental objects or qualities[165]

Self-Determinism

We can deliberate consciously about our circumstances and enact those behaviors that seem most likely to produce optimal results. I define self-determinism as *planning and enacting one's activities in accordance with one's declared purposes*. In practice, self-determinism includes careful consideration and application of one's motives, beliefs, and actions.

Morality dictates that we apply our most beneficent commitments (in addition to our selfish desires) to decide our actions. To illustrate this theme, Philosophers Andrew Brook and Robert J. Stainton described how self-determinism is applied in action:

I engage in a careful process of identifying alternative courses of action, relevant values I hold, my objectives, the interests and situations of others, my beliefs about how various alternatives will play out, and so on. These deliberations cause me to arrive at a certain decision.[166]

Metacognition and metamotivation empower us to accomplish our most challenging goals, such as completing a long and difficult negotiation to reach a consensus with someone (despite the frustration that may accompany such efforts), or creating a new enterprise even though we fear the risks. With practice, we can learn to create and accomplish increasingly difficult goals in succession.

> If we want to accomplish something important, we can decide to learn how to achieve it.

Taking Action

Methods for learning to work very well have been well documented. Ideal guidelines for self-management don't execute themselves; they need to be applied heuristically.

First, it's essential that we articulate our purposes and goals as clearly as possible. A goal (or a promise) is a specific result to be achieved within an explicit time limit.

Publicly declaring our intentions motivates us to behave in accordance with those commitments, and it also opens the possibility for others to support our endeavors. It's highly advantageous to clarify our objectives and share them with friends and colleagues who may support those aims, especially those who might offer to assist or provide useful advice.

Working with other people is facilitated by producing *conversations for action*, which are designed to produce results. Chilean engineer, philosopher, and politician Fernando Flores developed this theoretical framework for effective communication, noting that "certain speech acts, particularly requests, promises, offers, and declarations, serve as building blocks for activating commitments…"[167]

Table 7 contains Flores' descriptions of three ways of speaking that are particularly effective in producing highly successful communication.

Declaration	A speaker declares a new world of possibilities for action in a community.
Offer/Promise	A speaker offers or promises to take care of something that a listener is concerned about.
Request	A speaker asks a listener to take care of something that the speaker is concerned about.

Table 7. Elements of a conversation for action.[168]

Flores noted that two other types of utterances, *assertions* and *assessments*, are used to support action dialogues.

In response to a request, a listener might accept, decline, or generate a counteroffer (e.g., suggest a later deadline or nominate someone else who could perform the task).

These dialogical tools are quite simple, yet they're enormously powerful when they're applied by people who are cooperating to produce things together.

The benefits produced through conversations for action aren't limited to professional relationships. Effective communication and progressive dialogues may be applied to any cooperative work that people intend to accomplish.

Learning to flourish in social relationships requires participating in ethical discourses and actively caring for the well-being of others. We may benefit more from engaging in cooperative social relations than we do from withholding, evading, or prevaricating; relationships thrive when partners communicate authentically.

We can generate visions of a future that we want to create. We apply self-determinism by declaring possibilities for action, describing specifically what we intend to achieve, and learning how to produce it. We can organize our activities around making and keeping promises to perform actions that are consistent with accomplishing our most important objectives.

> *Declaring one's values* and *promising to achieve ambitious goals* represent two self-determined and interrelated discursive/regulative processes for managing one's affective, cognitive, and behavioral development. The more goals that we set and the harder we work to achieve them the more likely we are to succeed in our endeavors.

Emotions

People typically want to experience pleasurable feelings (such as joy and satisfaction) and to avoid feeling some others (like grief, shame, or fear).

We perceive, interpret, and react to what goes on around us according to our beliefs about what's good or bad for us. Our feelings are automatically (re)activated by events, which may trigger desires to participate or to flee.

Strong negative feelings may interfere with clear thinking, so it's usually best to refrain from negotiating a conflict (or making a significant decision) when we're upset. It's usually better to take a break from whatever's going on until our thoughts and feelings allow for calmer and deeper consideration. As noted on an Australian government health care website,

Negative emotions stop us from thinking and behaving rationally and seeing situations in their true perspective. When this occurs, we tend to see only what we want to see and remember only what we want to remember. This only prolongs the anger or grief and prevents us from enjoying life. The longer this goes on, the more set the problem becomes.[169]

In Chapter 4, I noted that we may repress our unpleasant emotions to avoid feeling them, but they nevertheless resonate as part of our human nature. We may distract ourselves with hobbies (such as social work, playing games, taking recreational drugs, or jumping out of airplanes), but such relief doesn't provide immunity from displeasure.

Over time, some events that we've experienced repeatedly have produced strong feelings. We know about these situations, we know how we feel about them, and we understand what to do about them. For example, I want to go to my favorite restaurant because I believe that they serve excellent meals at reasonable prices. I don't want to talk to my cousin because I believe (from observing her behavior for decades) that she's compelled to criticize me without reasonable justification.

Emotional *issues* (recurring bouts of distress) present serious difficulties for many of us, but it's possible to learn to reduce the severity and the frequency of one's distressful episodes. We can transform our lives by altering or abandoning our least coherent beliefs about ourselves and other people.

Psychotherapeutic support can be greatly beneficial for learning to adopt perspectives that facilitate well-being. Therapists can recommend practical methods to support people in achieving emotional balance, from meditation to exercise, affirmations, and managing one's expectations.[170]

According to the Health Encyclopedia from the University of Rochester Medical Center, "The best clue that it's time to see a therapist is a sense that the way you're thinking, feeling, or behaving is interfering with your normal life."[171]

As therapist Dan Mager noted,

Being out of balance emotionally usually involves *either* not allowing yourself to experience your feelings as they evolve by avoiding *or* suppressing them or being so attached to and identified with them that your feelings are all-consuming. Emotional balance occurs when we allow ourselves to feel whatever comes up, without stifling or being overwhelmed by it, and learn to accept our feelings without judgment.[172]

Accepting our most unpleasant feelings as an inescapable aspect of humanity may seem like a bitter pill to swallow, and it may be a difficult process to master (especially if they include helplessness and powerlessness). However, (as described in the section above on Diminishing Suffering) it's possible to manage our painful experiences through self-awareness.

The willingness to accept such experiences as they occur (rather than magnifying their intensity by dwelling on how bad we believe them to be) causes them to dissipate more quickly than they otherwise would. With practice, we can manage to suffer less and less.

We can *learn not to be upset about being upset*. Being afraid of being afraid,[173] or feeling ashamed about feeling ashamed,[174] exacerbates those feelings. We dispel those feelings by accepting them and by expressing them to sympathetic listeners.

Many people are very judgmental about emotional self-expression in social settings. As a child, I was repeatedly warned against expressing strong negative emotions in most circumstances (because it's often considered impolite). Eventually, I figured out that we can share our worst feelings in a "safe" environment – when we're with people who won't condemn us for expressing what we feel. We can learn to suppress our fury and disgust about what goes on around us until it's safe to communicate them.[175]

Managing Intrapersonal Conflict

Individual (*intrapersonal*) conflict occurs within our own minds when our ideas (or emotions) are mixed. Sometimes we're not clear about what to do because our options seem equally desirable (or undesirable).

Since thinking and feeling are interdependent, cognitive and emotional conflicts often occur at the same time.

Is consummating a strong emotional attraction to a third party a good reason for deserting one's family? Some people have made that choice. Is stealing from one's neighbor more important than living without a television set? It might be so if one hates one's neighbor.

Cognitive dissonance ("psychological conflict resulting from incongruous beliefs and attitudes held simultaneously"[176]) motivates us to do anything that we can to reduce the emotional discomfort produced by mental strife.[177]

We might be confused about important decisions that have long-term consequences: get divorced, or work at producing a better marriage? Retire early, or continue working to save more money?

Less important decisions are also subject to conflict resolution when our values clash with one another. In planning today's dinner, I consider both my commitment to maintaining health (eating nutritious foods) and my desire to enjoy my meal. This is a balancing act that includes considerations of what I ate yesterday and what I might eat tomorrow.

We might need to fulfill a particular purpose at the cost of failing to fulfill others. If two urgent situations occur simultaneously, we need to judge which activity should take precedence.

> Resolving intrapersonal conflict isn't simply a matter of knowing which actions are always right or wrong. It's about discernment: producing well-justified assessments in each situation while taking values and contextual factors into account.

Moral discernment requires rigorous thinking and careful judgment regarding what's fair or good for people in particular situations. That's why our decisions should include consideration of contextual factors, and that's why systems of jurisprudence have evolved into highly complex discourses (which are subject to revision).

Sometimes, value conflicts mean choosing between life and death. Social *solidarity*[178] might be judged to outweigh all other values, even survival, as when soldiers decide to sacrifice their lives to save others.

It may sometimes be exceedingly difficult to decide what to do. Mental conflict may produce distress, from mild to deeply painful. However, we can manage the influence of emotionality by applying practical wisdom in deciding how we ought to behave.

In the preceding pages, I've presented a story about applying values to create purposes, setting goals, and then working hard (in collaboration with others) to achieve results. Unfortunately, this scheme doesn't provide a prescription for success in life; it doesn't tell us which commitments to create, which goals to set, or how to learn to accomplish the things that we intend to achieve.

If we're not clear on what we need to do to be highly productive and deeply satisfied, then we're unlikely to be deeply fulfilled with any results that we achieve. To remedy that situation, we might consult with our social partners to establish our priorities and set our goals.

Changing Our Stories

Our lives' stories include the sets of opinions that we hold about ourselves.

If we're not very well satisfied with our success in life, we might be seeking greater fulfilment (or we might consider doing so). Since our habits of thinking and behaving may include beliefs and activities that produce more harm than benefit, we can learn to distinguish which ideas and practices we can discard or alter to produce better results.

We can rewrite the stories we've been living by developing new scripts to direct our future endeavors. That includes figuring out where we went wrong in the past and learning more productive methods to apply in our future practices.

Cultural History

We absorbed many basic beliefs from the people who taught us about life and language when we first learned about those things. We built our worldviews on these foundations.

Much of what we learned is acclaimed knowledge – widely accepted ("correct") beliefs and opinions upon which most thoughtful people agree. Nevertheless, some of the ideas that we've presumed to be certainly true may be unjustifiable.

When I was very young, I thought that my caregivers were telling me the absolute truth about the world and the people in it. Eventually, I discovered that I was mistaken about that.

True believers defend their faith (the stories they live by). If two people have learned conflicting versions of the absolute truth, it's practically impossible for them to reconcile their perspectives.

On the other hand, we can manage very well without absolute truths if we focus on the coherency of our discourses. We can decide which ideas are very well justified through observation and cogent (contextual) reasoning.

> If we realize that abstract descriptions of an object or an event may be more or less accurate but never completely true, then we can examine each idea to assess which explanations are more reasonable (that is, more justified) than others.

Some of us learned to live according to religious foundations, complete with ultimate authorities, cadres of clergy, and supposedly correct rules for being a "righteous" person and living a "good" life. Others learned a variety of different tales, such as the communist narrative about competing social classes.[179] Some people (perhaps those who received little care or attention when they were young) learned that they should take care of their own requirements without caring much about other peoples' needs.

While the cultural stories that we live by might not seem false to us, they do to those who disagree. The history of humankind is rife with social conflicts between people who struggle mightily to sustain and propagate their cultural identities. This situation results from disagreeing about which abstract beliefs are true when none of them could possibly be so.

It might be better for us to understand that no assertion about what's right for everyone or what everybody should do should be considered absolutely correct.

Personal Stories

We can't intentionally disbelieve what we believe or believe what we disbelieve. Our beliefs change when our perceptions conflict with them and we alter our views to make sense of the evidence that we observe.

Most of us want to be right (and be seen to be right) about what we think and do; this craving drives us to defend our beliefs and justify our actions. It's not always a conscious desire, but its strength and power aren't diminished by being unconscious.

We might think that our beliefs about ourselves must be true. If someone tells me something about me and I disagree, is it always appropriate to believe that they're mistaken?

Not necessarily! Some people understand human nature better than I do, and other people aren't subject to my personal biases in their interpretations of what I say or do.

If we want to change our habits (rewrite our stories, develop our identities), how do we learn to alter our habits of thinking and behaving? We begin by shifting our perspectives, that is, learning new ways to look at ourselves and our circumstances. As psychologist Wayne Dyer noted, "If you change the way you look at things, the things you look at change."[180]

> Experts in philosophy apply perspectives on linguistic meanings that are unfamiliar to most of us. Skilled psychologists comprehend the processes of thinking, feeling, and performing in ways that most people don't.

We can learn a great deal about how we function by accommodating what the wisest scholars and researchers in human history figured out about how people operate.[181]

It's not possible to predict what a thoughtful person can learn if one inquires deeply. It *is* possible to learn to alter the beliefs that have kept us stuck where we don't want to be.

Peak Experience and Peak Performance

Self-actualization represents the experience of doing what we ought to do while being authentically self-expressive.[182] It includes purpose and spontaneity, effortlessness, and meaningfulness.

One aspect of self-actualization is described by Maslow's notion of *peak experience,* a feeling of joy and well-being while in action, "a generalization for the best moments of human being, for the happiest moments of life, for experiences of ecstasy, rapture, bliss, of the greatest joy."[183]

Many researchers have investigated the experiences of contentment and well-being. For example, Hungarian-American psychologist Mihalyi Csikszentmihalyi suggested that we learn to cultivate (long-term) happiness by achieving control over the contents of our consciousness.[184]

Csikszentmihalyi also developed the idea of *flow* (or *peak performance*), the experience of identifying intensely with one's actions, without being distracted by the historical stories that plague us the rest of the time. He described this experience as

…an optimal experience…an end unto itself…the activity that consumes us becomes intrinsically rewarding…[Flow] lifts the course of life to a different level. Alienation gives way to involvement, enjoyment replaces boredom, helplessness turns into feelings of control…When experience is intrinsically rewarding life is justified in the present, instead of being held hostage to hypothetical future gain.[185]

Love and Intimacy

Love is considered by many as an important value, one that may (under appropriate conditions) be applied to our benefit. This subject has received a great deal of interest in human history.

One approach describes it as "strong affection for another," or "attraction based on sexual desire."[186] Affection and attraction are feelings, so by these definitions love is seen as a transient experience. No feeling is permanent… they all come and go in turn.

Love may also be seen as a more complex idea that has been called *divine* love, a deep appreciation for humanity and nature in general.[187]

When we describe our feelings, we represent them as abstract concepts (ideas). However, feelings don't lend themselves to very specific definitions; for example, we may distinguish various types of fear.[188]

We label our experiences so that we can communicate them, but the words we use to describe them are insufficient to denote their complexity. Simply saying I'm feeling love doesn't describe much about my emotion; it doesn't communicate its significance to me, nor its effects on my behavior.

There's no true description of what loving or being loved should mean. Like every other ideal value, its implications and applications must be worked out as we go along.

The abstract value of *intimacy* is often associated with *romantic* love. However, intimacy may also refer to a wide range of interpersonal relations (emotional, intellectual, physical, spiritual…).[189]

One notable form of relating is a *pair bond*. We may tend to seek comfort and approval by relating closely with someone who cares enough about us to support us in being well and becoming more fulfilled.

If we appreciate love as an ideal value, rather than a feeling, then our relationship with it shifts. If we intend to apply it in our lives (on purpose), then we need to learn how to be someone who loves…despite the fact that feelings come and go.

As the notion of divine love indicates, loving may become a habit, and it may serve as a practical way to operate.

Feeling love is fine of course, but applying love can mean much more than feeling good about someone or having highly pleasurable interactions. Like joyfulness, the ideal of loving may be applied in many ways. Like joy, we can learn to bring it to life.

If we think that we know for certain what love (or intimacy) should be like for us, then we lock ourselves into an imaginary picture of an ideal state that's impossible to manifest in practice. Worse, we might require that others adopt our standards before we can relate very well with them.

> Our experiences of interpersonal matters can hardly match our ideal pictures of what we want our social life to be. If we believe that our feelings should correspond exactly to our ideals, then we're mistaken, and we're bound to be disappointed.

Chapter 7
Communication and Relationship

Effective Communication

Social flourishing is developed by improving our communication skills and increasing our levels of cooperation with others. Concern for other people's values, beliefs, and intentions is of primary importance in developing flourishing relationships.

If we intend to relate very well with anyone, we should support their well-being (security, comfort, pleasure, etc.) as well as our own, and assist them whenever we can.

In practice, we can develop highly effective and productive methods for communicating. This includes adapting to the needs of the people we're with; the better we do that, the better we can relate and cooperate.

When my spouse and I decided to become partners, we promised each other that we would resolve every interpersonal issue or disagreement by *discussing and adjusting our perspectives* until we could agree on what was best for both of us. The purpose of these conversations is to figure out how to manage (balance) our individual needs and desires so that we can both be as well satisfied as our circumstances allow.

Our pact obligates us to be objectively reasonable (as well as we can!) in examining every operational issue, *and every psychological obstacle* (feeling, desire, belief, attitude, or compulsion) that prevents either of us from being fulfilled.

In the process, we discovered that every barrier to interpersonal harmony that we face results from the *insistent* need to fulfill some desire or other. This (mild) form of egoism doesn't claim that one's own needs are always paramount, just that one's current desire happens to be of supreme importance at that moment.

In practice, that attitude manifests as "I *need* to do (or to have) *this* – which you don't want me to do (or have);" or "I need you to do something (that you don't want to do)."

What are the alternatives for dealing with these circumstances? If we can't both get exactly what we want, then how can we both manage to be satisfied? These are the questions to be resolved when facing interpersonal conflicts with a committed partner.

Our satisfaction with our relationships depends upon how our beliefs and opinions enable or prevent full cooperation and highly effective communication. Some of our ideas about how we should or shouldn't work with someone may prevent us from relating as well as we'd like.

> Our beliefs and attitudes determine the limits of our satisfaction with a relationship. If our ideas are incoherent or if we insist on having our way, we're unlikely to relate very well.

Resolving Interpersonal Conflict

Interpersonal disputes are common, and we may work to resolve or mitigate them when they arise.

Unresolved disputes don't vanish. As noted by psychological counselor Brian Gersho,

Learning to manage and tolerate our differences, rather than letting them fester and cause increased resentment with each passing year, is a critical step to promote a satisfying long-term relationship.[190]

Open-minded and reasonable argumentation is essential to working through interpersonal differences. That process is applied by reviewing evidence, contexts, and alternative perspectives.

> If social partners are committed to resolving interpersonal conflicts, then they may engage in progressive dialogues to decide upon mutually agreeable resolutions.

Moral standards differ from region to region and from person to person, and ideas about the meanings of our actions vary according to individual interpretations. Even when we agree in theory on moral values (such as fairness or kindness), we might sometimes disagree about which specific actions are indicated or contraindicated (what's kinder or fairer) in particular situations.

It's simpler to do whatever we want instead of considering the effects of our actions on others, but working well with people requires the willingness to cooperate in deciding what should be done.

Certainty bias may prevent us from admitting that we might be mistaken even when we can't prove that we're correct. This reluctance may interfere with authentic communication and conflict resolution.

It might be extremely painful even to consider the possibility that one has been mistaken about something important and has been repeating that mistake for a long time. Fear of being shamefully wrong may prevent us from adjusting our ideas and resolving conflicts. Sometimes people aren't willing to resolve a conflict unless they understand that doing so would advance their own purposes.

Evading and prevaricating may be combined with righteous insistence to avoid discussing which ideas are more reasonable than others. It's possible to belittle, dominate, and/or disparage others rather than resolve our differences.

Mutual satisfaction requires that people place more emphasis on reasoning than they do on insisting. The idea of *practical reason* indicates that reflecting on what to think produces more coherent perspectives (and more appropriate actions) than reacting thoughtlessly.

Practical reason is the general human capacity for resolving, through reflection, the question of what one is to do. Deliberation of this kind is practical in at least two senses. First, it is practical in its subject matter, insofar as it is concerned with action. But it is also practical in its consequences or its issue, insofar as reflection about action itself directly moves people to act.[191]

Decision theory is the study of how people make choices. As described by philosopher R. Jay Wallace in *The Stanford Encyclopedia of Philosophy*,

Decision theory…becomes an all-encompassing framework for understanding free human behavior, according to which all agents who act freely are striving to produce outcomes that would be optimal, relative to their current preferences and beliefs.[192]

If people disagree about how to deal with practical matters, it may be possible to negotiate what should or shouldn't be done. However, when people disagree about abstract ideas and principles, then differences of opinion may be impossible to resolve.

For example, I might believe that it's morally wrong to kill animals for food or to buy meat to feed my family. In that case, it's practically impossible to reconcile my position with that of someone who has always believed that there's nothing immoral in eating meat.

Conflict resolution is facilitated when people realize that it's not appropriate to try to get everything that we desire. Sometimes it's more important to provide what someone else needs rather than get what we want.

Competition Vs. Cooperation

An essential dimension of relating with people is the ratio of competition to cooperation. Competition describes a situation where people strive for dominance, while cooperation is a more egalitarian approach to communicating and relating.

Cooperation facilitates self-development and social flourishing. In theory, cooperative communication enables us to work well together; in practice, this requires paying close attention to supporting each other's purposes and goals.

Competition is ubiquitous in human society. Most young people learn to compete early in life (perhaps against their own siblings at first), and rivalry is prevalent in adulthood. Many people seem to want to dominate or control others whenever they sense an opportunity to do so.

If we dislike someone's actions for private reasons, we might manifest antagonistic attitudes, contradict them without coherent justification, or reject them as inferior and unworthy of our attention. These are common (though nefarious) methods for demonstrating one's supposed superiority.

In contrast, the egalitarian approach to relating grants equal power to partners who intend to work together.

It may be very difficult to break a lifelong habit of promoting one's own superiority. If one is accustomed to operating competitively with others, how can one learn to behave differently?

In theory, commitments to cooperation, negotiation, and solidarity may produce optimally complete and authentic communication. In practice, communicating as well as we can is sometimes quite challenging. Our psychological defense mechanisms produce competitive attitudes in many situations.[193]

Maintaining a commitment to behaving cooperatively is relatively easy for those who learned to do so at an early age and are committed to cooperation and solidarity. However, authoritative domination is customary in many cultures, such as religious communities, military organizations, and totalitarian governments – these situations aren't designed to support the possibility of full cooperation.

Some of us might habitually strive to demonstrate that we're highly competent thinkers and communicators.[194] Psychologist Saif Farooqi summarized the insights of Austrian physician and psychiatrist Alfred Adler (a pioneer in the study of human psychology) to describe how (and why) people may strive to dominate.

[Alfred] Adler suggested that striving for superiority is the final goal of all humankind. It unifies personality and makes all behaviours comprehensible. Adler also suggested that striving for superiority is a way to compensate the feelings of inferiority and weakness. People are always pushed by the need to overcome inferiority and pulled by the desire for completion and wholeness.[195]

In theory, flourishing relationships require a mutual commitment to constructive values such as coherency, morality, and flexibility. In practice, cooperative communication requires that we apply these values in action.

The Third Entity

One of the keys to relating optimally is the understanding that an interpersonal relationship is an entity unto itself, a distinct object that people intentionally construct together. This means that three entities are involved rather than two, and it means that what's best for *us* (the third entity) takes precedence when working together.

A relationship (like a plant or a car) needs attention, which occurs when the participants focus on what's needed to nurture a thriving affiliation. If one of my houseplants is dying, I must attend to it or lose it. If my car breaks down, I'll arrange my schedule to get it repaired as soon as I can.

If a friend is in trouble, I'll drop everything else to help.

Cultivating a relationship implies that we must sometimes negotiate conditions for both of us to be as satisfied as we can manage. For example, if I'm discussing with my spouse about when we should take a vacation (she wants to go soon; I'd rather wait a month or two) or where we should go, we should first examine all the operational factors: we should analyze the objective reasons (such as managing our budget and our other responsibilities) which would favor one option or another.

If we find no strong evidence that indicates which choice is better for *us,* it becomes essential either for one of us to accommodate the other's desire, or else to negotiate a third (mutually acceptable) plan.

We can each indulge the other's desires on different occasions. The values of generosity and fairness may be applied liberally to facilitate workability.

Creating Progressive Dialogues

Supporting people often includes working to fulfil their purposes. This intention may be applied in each of our conversations.

> A highly successful relationship is built upon a foundation of mutual support, which requires a clear and consistent commitment from each partner.

It's worth noting that the idea of a 'partner' isn't limited to our closest allies. Any serious conversation may be seen as a form of partnership that demands cooperation.

Even if we understand that practical wisdom refers to applying coherency and morality in practice by declaring beneficent commitments and manifesting them in action, resolving interpersonal conflicts in daily life may pose difficult challenges.

For example, engaging in conversations that challenge our beliefs may be difficult. Even if we're clear that most of our language is highly abstract and can only be grounded in objectivity through operational measures, it still might be quite painful to re-examine our cognitive structures for coherency – especially if they're actually mistaken!

> Communicating and relating very well is facilitated by applying metacognitive self-correction.

Strong emotions may interfere with our effectiveness in applying critical analysis and reasonable justification. We might prefer to avoid discussing our differences, but resolving serious conflicts usually requires arguing and negotiating.

We might hold preconceptions about our competence in negotiating effectively. If we don't believe that we can resolve our conflicts together, then certainty bias and self-fulfilling prophecy will prevent us from doing so.

After we've thought things through and discussed them as reasonably as we can with a mutual commitment to resolving an issue, we might still be unclear about what to do. We might work together for hours or days and not reach a resolution about what's best for the third entity (a flourishing relationship). If we've given our best efforts and still don't know how to proceed, then we might seek the support of a wise mediator who might describe some perspectives that neither of us had considered.

Beyond Ego

Individual fulfillment is instrumental to social flourishing. If one's basic needs aren't met, fulfillment is impossible and social interaction is severely compromised.

Yet, contentment doesn't guarantee social success. Many people whose individual needs are well satisfied haven't learned to relate very well with others.

Pleasure and joy (delight, elation, bliss, or ecstasy) are feelings that people want to experience. We can enjoy ourselves alone, but good feelings are multiplied when people experience them together.

Sometimes one's well-being depends on working with someone else. The road from self-involvement (our natural state at birth) to achieving remarkable success in social relationships involves developing one's social intelligence.[196]

Social skills can be improved on purpose through a commitment to learning. As Canadian writer Shannon Terrell suggests, "Strengthening and supporting your interpersonal intelligence can help you become an excellent communicator."[197]

When children are raised in a closed society (where caregivers describe other groups as inferior, antagonistic, or evil), it may be exceedingly difficult for them to learn a different approach to social behavior. In practice, we may assess (in numerous ways) how well people succeed in relating and communicating with each other, but there's no single or acclaimed method for doing that.[198]

Teamwork is about producing benefits for all team members. A Canadian government website describes habits that should be avoided in team environments (listed in Table 8).

Keeping potentially helpful information to oneself
Interacting in a negative or indifferent manner
Ignoring the ideas and opinions of others
Assuming that if people had anything of value to share then they would say it without being asked
Working alone without any interaction
Working competitively to the detriment of the common goal

Table 8. Examples of poor teamwork[199]

Nationalism[200] and ethnocentrism[201] divide humanity into competitive groups. *Culturism* has been defined as "a form of discrimination on the grounds of cultural norms."[202] To manifest social flourishing in action, we may focus instead on solidarity [203] and egalitarianism.[204]

Cooperating

Oxfordlearnersdictionaries.com defines the term cooperation as "doing something together or…working together toward a shared aim."[205] This idea describes practices that facilitate communication, collaboration and teamwork.

If cooperation is important to us, then we ought to understand clearly how it's applied effectively in practice, and we should distinguish when it's being disregarded. Table 9 depicts some attitudes and actions that indicate whether people are manifesting cooperation in practice.

	Cooperation	Non-Cooperation
Attitudes	Listening	Pretending to listen
	Supporting	Antagonizing
	Caring	Pretending to care while pursuing a personal agenda
	Trusting	Distrusting
	Addressing issues	Addressing personality characteristics
	Negotiating	Insisting
Actions	Communicating clearly	Obfuscating, lying, deceiving, dissembling, evading
	Communicating relevant ideas	Distracting
	Interjecting	Overriding
		Accusing, derogating
		Disrupting

Table 9. Contrasting communication practices.

British philosopher H. Paul Grice noted that cooperation is the basis of effective communication. His *Cooperative Principle for Communication* specifies how to produce useful conversations: say what's required to denote what you mean; don't say more than that; say it when it's required and in such a way that it can be clearly understood.[206]

> When it's important for communication to be effective, we should provide only relevant information and well-justified assertions while avoiding ambiguous or obscure language.

To resolve difficulties in understanding each other, we must determine how closely our interpretations correspond to the meanings that someone is denoting. Diligent listening includes recognizing where people's perspectives are closely congruent with our own and where their interpretations differ from ours. Clarification may be required before we can understand each other very well.

Listening serves another important function besides interpreting the meanings of words and sentences. We listen for meanings, but we can also sense people's intentions, which are signaled by their attitudes. For example, when we notice that someone has no intention of communicating cooperatively, we should understand that a mutually satisfactory conversation is very unlikely to be achieved.

Ways of Communicating

Some forms of communication are strictly whimsical, recreational, or arbitrary, but we often communicate because we want or need to get something done.

Expressing ourselves enables us to share our feelings, our ideas, and our intentions with each other. Effective communication is authentic communication – it reveals what we actually think and feel.

If it's extremely important to relate well with people, then cooperative communication practices are called for. To relate very well with others, it's important to reflect on a) how effectively (and how benevolently) we're sharing ourselves and b) how well we're listening.

We have many ideas and intentions, which sometimes conflict with each other. We're not always clear in our own minds about what we want at a particular moment. Even if we know what we want and say it authentically while committed to cooperating, we can hardly express everything that's behind what we're saying.

Our *meaning perspectives* (points of view) are indicated by our beliefs and our opinions. People with similar backgrounds share many viewpoints and can usually understand each other quite well. On the other hand, comprehending the ideas of people who have learned to interpret and evaluate things differently from oneself might be quite difficult.

Even when people share similar backgrounds, their communication styles may vary widely. Many of us aren't deeply committed to authentic self-expression, coherent reasoning, or benevolent action. Some people believe that it's natural and appropriate to dominate others whenever they can. False representation is a way of life for some, to whom looking good and feeling superior are more important than *integrity* ("the quality of being honest and having strong moral principles that you refuse to change"[207]).

As described in the previous section, competition (domination) may be more important than caring about other people's needs. Getting one's own way by any available means may sometimes be more important than anything else.[208]

Journalist Nathan J. Robinson described this aspect of human nature.

> The competitive urge is a destructive and sociopathic urge – it means total dedication to one's own success and a desire to prevent that of others. The spheres in which this is useful need to be carefully delimited…I certainly do not want to spend much of my time coming up with new ways to try to be better than other people…[209]

In practice, it's quite easy to distinguish antagonistic tactics from cooperative ones. When relating very well with someone isn't a priority because it's more important to achieve something for oneself, then uncooperative conversational tactics may be employed.

Expressing ourselves clearly and completely is only half the job of communicating effectively. If we intend to relate very well with people whose experiences differ from our own, then it's necessary to learn what they understand. Caring about what others think, listening closely to them, and thoughtfully considering their perspectives are equally important as expressing ourselves well.

Caring

Caring might be defined as an emotion, but it also refers to a wide variety of practical actions and activities. *In practice, caring is manifested by actively attending to other people's needs and desires.*

Social flourishing is determined by the qualities of our relationships. If we intend to relate well, then we should actively tend to other people's needs as well as our own.

> Strong beneficent commitments, combined with thoughtful consideration, facilitate optimal communication and flourishing relationships.

A classic example of caring is the relationship between a loving mother and her helpless baby. Caring mothers are very solicitous of their children's health and welfare, and they often put the needs of their children ahead of their own.

The activities involved in taking care of others' needs are essential elements in developing healthy relationships. It's difficult or impossible to relate or communicate very well with someone who pays little attention to what others want or need.

Empathy facilitates relating with other people. It's much easier to care for others and communicate effectively with them if we understand what they're going through.

There's no specific formula for succeeding at dealing with other people; that depends upon individual motives and local circumstances. However, it seems clear that considering what other people need or want should be a factor in making decisions that affect them.

Judging People

Many people have clearly demonstrated appalling habits that have produced very harmful consequences, and it's quite correct to believe that their actions should be considered as wrong. However, it's quite easy to issue biased derogatory judgments about people's actions without reasonable justification.

We react automatically to what we see people do; we may make snap judgments about the meanings of their actions. If we think that we should police someone else's morals, then we might react by criticizing their actions in antagonistic ways.

Yet, it's possible to do that without any reasonable moral justification, based solely on subjective opinions and an intention to dominate.

We can attempt to demonstrate that we're superior to other people by insisting that their actions are wrong, or that their personalities are *bad*. We can apply harsh judgments against anybody at any time *without any clear evidence* for our assertions. This common habit makes cooperative communication impossible.

As clinical psychologist Gregg Henriques pointed out,

> …someone is being judgmental when their judgments are power-driven, unempathetic, based on their own idiosyncratic values or tastes, overly based on other people's character, and are closed, shallow, and pessimistic, and ultimately have the consequence of making the other person feel problematically diminished.[210]

Philosopher Caroline J. Simon describes that process as deeply counterproductive to social relating, writing,

Being judgmental distorts our perception of other people, of ourselves, and of what matters most in living a well-lived human life. It feeds on and engenders a lack of sympathetic understanding of others. It is often linked with other related character flaws: hypocrisy, self-righteousness, malice, insensitivity, and the enjoyment of destructive gossip.[211]

Applying Flexibility in Action

If one is committed to learning, then open-mindedness is extremely important. A disposition toward cognitive flexibility enables self-correction and deep learning.

It's easy to discern people's interest in learning something; all we need to do is observe how closely they're listening to what they're hearing. Open-minded attitudes are quite easy to distinguish by noticing how long people actually consider what they're hearing before they respond, and by whether they're asking questions about something that they want to learn.

Of course, if one is devoted to maintaining what one already believes, then learning isn't an issue and there's no use in listening to people explain other perspectives!

Equity

Dictionary.com defines 'equity' as "fairness; impartiality."[212] *Fairness* refers to "…treating people equally or in a way that is reasonable,"[213] and *justice* is "the fair treatment of people."[214]

According to the *Stanford Encyclopedia of Philosophy*, egalitarianism demands that "People should be treated as equals, should treat one another as equals, should relate as equals."[215]

Balancing our needs with those of others is an essential activity when it comes to applying wisdom in practice. Producing fairness in action may require considering people's ideas, reconsidering one's beliefs, and accommodating other people's needs as well as we can manage.

Equity is instrumental to social flourishing. If we're deeply committed to applying justice in action, then we'll avoid behaving as if someone is less worthy of being treated fairly than someone else.

Workability: Consensus and Consent

The adjective *workable* refers to "(…a system, an idea, etc.) that can be used successfully and effectively."[216] The ideal value of *workability* may be used to describe how well we flourish in our relationships.

We can apply the idea of social workability operationally by observing what people do. *Optimal* workability (*consensus*) occurs when people agree on what to do and how to do it. Obviously, that situation facilitates productivity. It might occur without much discussion, or it might require some conversation to clarify our intentions and our methods.

Intermediate workability (*consent*) occurs when a partner simply accepts one's actions or plans (applying tolerance or indulgence). If my life partner wants to do something that doesn't harm anyone, I have no reasonable grounds for attempting to dissuade her (even if I'd prefer for her to something else).

No workability (*unworkability*) results when there's no consensus, no consent, and cooperation is out of the question.

In theory, workability requires that we communicate and cooperate well. In practice, it may be assessed according to how satisfied we (and our partners) are with our interactions.

We can also assess workability in real time by noticing how much support we generate for each other's purposes and goals. Ultimately, workability may be evaluated according to what we accomplish together.

Dealing with Antagonism

Our attitudes are determined by our beliefs and our feelings. Antagonism (*aggression* or *hostility*) is an attitude that may be produced by disapproval of people's actions. It may be associated with experiences of antipathy (resentment, anger, bitterness, etc.).

We're (more or less) cooperative or antagonistic at a given moment according to our beliefs, our feelings, and our circumstances. We might switch back and forth from antagonism to cooperation during a conversation.

As American educator Kendra Cherry wrote about aggression,

Aggression can serve a number of different purposes, including:

> Expressing anger or hostility
> Asserting dominance

Intimidating or threatening
Achieving a goal
Expressing possession
Responding to fear
Reacting to pain
Competing with others [217]

If I have a history of conflict with someone, then I may tend to perceive their utterances as antagonistic rather than cooperative and respond likewise. Bias and self-fulfilling prophecy may apply; if I believe that someone's attitude toward me is uncooperative, confirmation bias leads me to interpret their actions as such. To confirm my belief, I need only provoke them a little bit, and their (automatic) reactions are likely to validate my belief that their actions are hostile.

I might even think (or proclaim) that I behaved very well and that the conflicts were either a) unavoidable, or b) entirely their fault.

> Working cooperatively together is facilitated by being aware that cognitive biases prevent us from being fully objective, and by actively self-regulating our beliefs and our attitudes.

Guilt, Shame, Blame and Resentment

Guilt (culpability) refers to an assessment that someone has done something that is considered bad or wrong.

Shame is a feeling of humiliation that may arise when one judges oneself guilty of a transgression. If one is committed to moral responsibility, then shame is a sign that one's misdeed should be corrected (if possible).

Blame is an attitude associated with assigning guilt. It might rebound; if someone feels that they've been blamed unjustly, they may experience resentment as a result and they might blame the blamer for their critical attitude.

Even though shame is a useful indication that we understand and care about morality, it's usually considered an undesirable feeling, so we might do what we can to avoid it.

One option for avoiding shame is adopting egoism by deciding that the notion of morality is irrelevant. The Mayo Clinic describes *anti-social personality disorder* as "a mental health condition in which a person consistently shows no regard for right and wrong and ignores the rights and feelings of others."[218]

Another way to avoid feeling ashamed is to generate an attitude of pure righteousness, according to which we consider our justifications for our behavior to be perfectly adequate. For example, "I'm not ashamed that I hit my wife. She provoked me!"

The long-term effects of shame can be crippling. As psychotherapist Jeff Peterson noted,

The consequences of shame can be devastating and may lead to long-term risk-taking behaviors and suicidality. Chronic self-worth issues and relationship problems all reflect attachment challenges experienced by individuals responding to shame. In addition, the compounding effects of shame have the potential to lead to co-morbid disorders and maladaptive coping skills resulting in chronic physical and mental health problems.[219]

Therapist Stacy Wald recommends that the effects of chronic shame can be counteracted by responding appropriately:

Make an action plan to overcome areas in which shame is blocking your personal growth.

This plan could include the following:

- Engaging in positive self-talk (e.g. I deserve to be loved. I'm worthy.)
- Working on being more assertive (not aggressive)
- Developing a healthy support system of people who will accept you for who you are
- Letting go of the things you can't control or change
- Working toward forgiveness, acceptance, and love of yourself
- Speaking with a therapist to help you work through your feelings of shame.[220]

The long-term effects of *resentment* may also be psychologically debilitating. As relationship counselor Steven Stosny pointed out,

Resentment rarely goes away on its own...The habitual nature of resentment means that it is never specific to one behavior – nobody resents just one thing – and that its content is rarely forgotten. Instead, each new incident of perceived unfairness automatically links onto previous ones, eventually forging a heavy chain.[221]

The object of one's resentment is much less (if at all) affected than the one who's indignant. As South African political leader Nelson Mandela pointed out, "Resentment is like drinking poison and then hoping it will kill your enemies."[222]

Fortunately, the effects of long-term resentment can be mitigated or overcome. Having suffered greatly from that emotion, I was relieved to learn that there's an antidote to this feeling: cultivating and applying the value of forgiveness.

We can't forgive someone and resent them at the same time. However, indignation tends to recur, so forgiveness isn't a one-time resolution. When resentment reappears, the option of forgiving remains available.

According to the experts at mayoclinic.org,

Forgiveness…involves an intentional decision to let go of resentment and thoughts of revenge.

The act that hurt or offended you might always be with you, but forgiveness can lessen its grip on you and help free you from the control of the person who harmed you. Forgiveness can even lead to feelings of understanding, empathy, and compassion for the one who hurt you.

Forgiveness doesn't mean forgetting or excusing the harm done to you or making up with the person who caused the harm. Forgiveness brings a kind of peace that helps you go on with life…

Getting another person to change isn't the point of forgiveness. It's about focusing on what you can control in the here and now. Think of forgiveness more about how it can change your life by bringing you peace, happiness, and emotional and spiritual healing. Forgiveness can take away the power the other person continues to have in your life.[223]

Social Consciousness

The future of our species depends on reversing the disastrous consequences that human activities have inflicted on our planet's biosphere. A great deal of political and social action will be required for that to happen.

Yet, as noted by American educator Dustin Axe, many (perhaps most) of us are so preoccupied with our individual interests that we can't look beyond them to deal with broader social issues. Those of us who are familiar with the political struggles that afflict human civilization may feel powerless in the face of the historical forces that threaten to overwhelm us.

Many people are completely unaware of social injustices in their community and they are complacent toward major challenges facing the planet. They take an active role of ignorance and entitlement, and they are apathetic toward poverty, war, and climate change. They lack enthusiastic political beliefs, and few have meaningful interests or convictions. This is what it means to be socially unconscious.[224]

We might feel overburdened by our individual needs. As Axe noted, "It is easy to ignore problems in the community when one has problems of their own."[225]

In contrast, some people have spent their lives working to fulfill the basic needs of those who lack the means to do so.

In 1907, American sociologist Charles H. Cooley published an article in *The American Journal of Sociology* in which he suggested that the human mind is a collective phenomenon, and that each individual mind is a small part of this "organic whole." He wrote that our thoughts are "linked" with those who came before us and those around us.[226]

While we may understand that individuals are separate from each other, Cooley suggested that this perspective "springs from a failure to grasp adequately the social nature of all higher consciousness…The social ideas that I have are closely connected with those that other people have."[227]

Cooley noted that those who lack social awareness are unaware of the "conditions upon which [social injustice and its evil consequences] depend and of the means by which they may be redressed,"[228] and are therefore powerless to mitigate them.

Cooley was optimistic about the emergence of social consciousness into human nature, but in the century since he published his article the threats to human society have multiplied. We've begun to show hopeful signs of attending to global issues, but we're far from united on this project.

Nationalism and ethnocentrism continue to prevail widely, and individual citizens have little power to affect these deeply rooted perspectives.

Social consciousness begins with commitments to human solidarity and beneficence toward others.

> If we don't recognize the importance of moral values, we can't apply them in action. If we appreciate them, then we can work to manifest them in our practices.

Some academic research has been provided to explain social consciousness in terms of its operational distinctions. For example, sociologists Marilyn Mandala Schlitz, Cassandra Vieten, and Elizabeth M. Miller formulated a theoretical hierarchy (summarized in Table 10) to describe five ways of experiencing one's relationship with social issues.

1. Embedded	presocial consciousness; no awareness of social, cultural, and biological factors.
2. Self-Reflexive	appreciation of the effects of social factors on one's consciousness; begin to analyze our own biases and remove our perceptual blinders
3. Social	forming the intention to contribute to the well-being of others; increasing comprehension and appreciation of other people's perspectives.
4. Collaborative Social	working with others to produce solutions (collaborative action to effect changes).
5. Resonant	experiencing interconnectedness and rapport with others.

Table 10. Levels of Individual and social consciousness.[229]

Level 1 resembles Axe's description of social unconsciousness. Level 2 describes the realization that we're constrained by cognitive beliefs and emotional processes that limit our perspectives. Those who attain level 2 may decide to investigate ways of thinking and habits of action that are unfamiliar, which may lead to appreciating possibilities for engaging in social action (levels 3 and 4). Supporting the well-being of other people may produce level 5 experiences: identifying and communicating with others on equal terms.

We can encourage the next generation to work on rehabilitating our biosphere and ameliorating the political pandemonium which plagues human society. We may note that many young people who understand what needs to be done have already stepped up to the front lines of public controversy.

One famous example is Malala Yousafzai, an Afghan student who in 2012, at age fifteen, was shot in the head to punish her for attending school. She recovered to lead a grassroots movement that promotes women's rights around the world, and she vowed that "every day I fight to ensure all girls receive 12 years of free, safe, quality education."[230]

We may also be inspired by Swedish environmental activist Greta Thunberg, who in September 2019 (at sixteen years of age) assailed world leaders at the United Nation's Climate Action Summit in New York City, declaring,

People are suffering. People are dying. Entire ecosystems are collapsing. We are in the beginning of a mass extinction, and all you can talk about is money and fairy tales of eternal economic growth…For more than 30 years, the science has been clear. How dare you continue to look away and come here saying that you're doing enough when the politics and solutions needed are still nowhere in sight.[231]

We might decide to spend some of our time working with others who are committed to resolving problematic issues in our communities. While social action has always been available as an avenue for wealthy people to contribute to others, there's never been a more urgent need for people everywhere to collaborate in winning the Battle for Planet Earth.

We may adopt new habits voluntarily, and we'll eventually be forced to adapt to legislation.

Many scientists, sociologists, and politicians are designing innovative technologies and new legislation to preserve the healthy parts of our ecosystem and repair the damaged ones. It remains to be seen how well (and how quickly) they can manage to accomplish this task.

The contributions of the next generations of humans will be crucial; however, our educational systems aren't very well equipped to support today's children in learning to become thoughtful and wise adults.

Sternberg recommended in 2001 that explicit instruction in thinking skills should be provided in schools at all levels of education.[232] He denoted sixteen principles for teaching wisdom, which include demonstrating the benefits of thinking outside of one's own needs and interests, role modeling, reading about wise judgments, teaching the use of independent thinking, recognizing other people's interests, and identifying the common good.

A curriculum that focuses on those techniques can be designed to promote social consciousness and may inspire people to adopt lifestyles that include all of those practices.

As Australian educator Peter Ellerton suggested,

There are a variety of approaches to developing courses in critical thinking though it's preferable that critical thinking pedagogies are used in the delivery of all subjects. In this comprehensive model, students are taught the explicit skills of thinking as they learn their discipline knowledge.[233]

If appropriate educational materials become available, educators and university administrators may eventually produce curricula that will inspire future generations of teachers to learn the basic elements of wisdom and apply them in practice. Producing that objective may require political and social action by groups of citizens who recognize the potential benefits of reforming education in that respect.[234]

Acknowledgments

My appreciation for my partner, Michelle Kusters, is unconstrained. Our collaboration made this work possible.

I was extremely fortunate to have studied with two brilliant scholars, Vladimir Zeman and Kai Nelson. Their perspectives, inherited from the wisest philosophers in history, inspired me to produce this book.

Notes

_____

Introduction

[1]https://www.psychologytoday.com/ca/blog/practical-wisdom/201012/practical-wisdom-the-right-way-to-do-the-right-thing-0

[2]https://www.theatlantic.com/health/archive/2012/08/does-wisdom-bring-happiness-or-vice-versa/260949/

[3]https://www.collinsdictionary.com/us/dictionary/english/wisdom

[4]https://www.oxfordlearnersdictionaries.com/us/definition/english/coherence?q=COHERENCE

[5]Noddings, N. (1984) Caring. Berkeley; Los Angeles, CA: University of California Press (p. 6).

[6]Sternberg, R. J. (2001) "Why schools should teach for wisdom: The balance theory of wisdom in educational settings," Educational Psychologist, 36, 227–245.

[7]See Chapter 1. This idea relates to the theory of scientific investigation: empiricism "the belief that people should

rely on practical experience and experiments, rather than on theories, as a basis for knowledge"
https://www.collinsdictionary.com/dictionary/english/empiricism

[8]Searching disciplines for producing fulfilment on Google returned 5.33million hits in 0.3 seconds

[9]Halpern, D. F. (2002) "Cognitive science and the work of reform," New Directions for Higher Education, 119, 41–43 (p. 41).

Chapter 1

[10]American educator Robert J. Sternberg defined wisdom as the "achievement of a common good through a balance among (a) intrapersonal, (b) interpersonal, and (c) extrapersonal interests, over the (a) short and (b) long terms…" Sternberg, R. J. (2001). Why schools should teach for wisdom: The balance theory of wisdom in educational settings. Educational Psychologist 36, 227–245.

https://www.tandfonline.com/doi/abs/10.1207/S15326985EP3604_2

[11]Feldman, R. 1998, "Charity, principle of" In: Routledge Encyclopedia of Philosophy, Taylor and Francis, viewed 25 December 2018, https://www.rep.routledge.com/articles/thematic/charity-principle-of/v-1 doi:10.4324/9780415249126-P006-1

[12]https://philosophyterms.com/empiricism

[13] Popper, K. (1972). Objective knowledge: an evolutionary approach. Oxford: The Clarendon Press (p. 75) (Emphasis added). It's worth noting that logic and arithmetic (so-called formal languages) refer only to abstract symbols. They don't refer directly to people or things in the world.

[14] https://en.wikiquote.org/wiki/Stephen_Hawking

[15] "a theory that it is impossible to attain absolutely certain empirical knowledge because the statements constituting it cannot be ultimately and completely verified" https://www.merriam-webster.com/dictionary/fallibilism

[16] See https://www.irishtimes.com/news/will-the-sun-rise-tomorrow-it-probably-will-but-we-don-t-know-for-sure-so-sunrise-cannot-be-guaranteed-from-a-scientific-viewpoint-1.190596

[17] See https://www.forbes.com/sites/michaeltnietzel/2019/08/26/a-college-reading-list-for-the-post-truth-era/

[18] https://www.oed.com/search/dictionary/?scope=Entries&q=justification

[19] Macdonald, H. (2018) Truth: How the Many Sides to Every Story Shape Our Reality. Little, Brown.

[20] Leviton, D.J. (2016). Weaponized Lies: How to Think Critically in the Post-Truth Era. New York, Dutton. (p. 13).

[21] https://www.yourdictionary.com/coherence. See also Young, James O., 'The Coherence Theory of Truth', The Stanford Encyclopedia of Philosophy (Summer 2024

Edition), Edward N. Zalta & Uri Nodelman (eds.). https://plato.stanford.edu/entries/truth-coherence

[22]Frankfurt, H. (2006). On Truth. Alfred A. Knopf (p. 100).

[23]Reiss, Julian and Jan Sprenger, 'Scientific Objectivity', The Stanford Encyclopedia of Philosophy (Winter 2020 Edition), Edward N. Zalta (ed.). https://plato.stanford.edu/archives/win2020/entries/scientific-objectivity

[24]Ibid

[25]https://www.britannica.com/science/cognitive-bias

[26]https://www.psychologytoday.com/ca/blog/your-brain-work/200910/hunger-certainty

[27]https://www.scientificamerican.com/article/the-certainty-bias/

[28]https://www.psychologytoday.com/ca/blog/science-choice/201504/what-is-confirmation-bias. It's been demonstrated that confirmation biased can be reduced through training. See https://phys.org/news/2024-01-cognitive-bias-decision.html

[29]Hegel, G. Phenomenology of Spirit. Translated by A.V. Miller. http://www.faculty.umb.edu/gary_zabel/Courses/Marxist_Philosophy/Hegel_and_Feuerbach_files/Hegel-Phenomenology-of-Spirit.pdf. (Emphasis added).

[30]Varga, Somogy and Guignon, Charles, "Authenticity,"

The Stanford Encyclopedia of Philosophy (Fall 2017 Edition), Edward N. Zalta (ed.) https://plato.stanford.edu/archives/fall2017/entries/authenticity

[31] The mothers might testify, but they might also lie

[32] Rawls, J. (1999) Collected Papers of John Rawls, ed. by Samuel Freeman, Cambridge, Mass.: Harvard University Press.

[33] Kuhn, T. (1962) The structure of scientific revolutions. Chicago, University of Chicago Press.

[34] merriam-webster.com defines social construct as "an idea that has been created and accepted by the people in a society" https://www.merriam-webster.com/dictionary/social%20construct

[35] https://www.iep.utm.edu/lang-phi/

[36] Biletzki, Anat and Matar, Anat, "Ludwig Wittgenstein," The Stanford Encyclopedia of Philosophy (Summer 2018 Edition), Edward N. Zalta (ed.). https://plato.stanford.edu/archives/sum2018/entries/wittgenstein/

[37] Popper, K. (1978). Three Worlds. The Tanner Lectures on Human Values, https://tannerlectures.org/wp-content/uploads/sites/105/2024/07/popper80.pdf

[38] Locke, J. (1850) An Essay Concerning Human Understanding, Book III Chapter X, part 15.

https://enlightenment.supersaturated.com/johnlocke/BOO

KIIIChapterX.html

[39] The leaders of this movement included Charles Peirce, James Dewey and William James

[40] Peirce wrote the pragmatic maxim: "Consider what effects, which might conceivably have practical bearings, we conceive the object of our conception to have. Then, our conception of those effects is the whole of our conception of the object." Legg, Catherine and Christopher Hookway, 'Pragmatism', The Stanford Encyclopedia of Philosophy (Summer 2021 Edition), Edward N. Zalta (ed.). https://plato.stanford.edu/entries/pragmatism/#PragMaxiPeir

[41] The Stanford Encyclopedia of Philosophy informs us that, "Operationalism is based on the intuition that we do not know the meaning of a concept unless we have a method of measurement for it." Chang, Hasok, 'Operationalism', The Stanford Encyclopedia of Philosophy (Fall 2021 Edition), Edward N. Zalta (ed.). https://plato.stanford.edu/archives/fall2021/entries/operationalism

Chapter 2

[42] https://www.sciencedirect.com/science/article/abs/pii/S221509191930015X

[43] https://encyclopedia.arabpsychology.com/metamotivation/

[44] See Chapter 6

[45] Frankfurt, H. (1971) "Freedom of the will," The Journal of Philosophy, LXVII. Reprinted in Geirsson, H. and Losonsky, M. (Eds.), Beginning metaphysics, 1998, pp. 407–421. https://www.sci.brooklyn.cuny.edu/~schopra/Persons/Frankfurt.pdf

[46] Some folks define tendency as an "inclination" to think or behave in particular ways. Applying philosophical pragmatism, I prefer operational definitions (which refer to observable actions).

[47] http://www.skilledatlife.com/why-planning-our-lives-is-important/ http://www.klientsolutech.com/how-planning-can-help-you-to-achieve-career-and-business-goals

[48] Aristotle (1962/2000) Nichomachean Ethics. Translated by Martin Ostwald (New York, NY: MacMillan/Library of the Liberal Arts, 1962). In F. E. Baird & W. Kaufmann (Eds.), Ancient philosophy (pp. 364–434). Upper Saddle River, NJ: Prentice Hall. (1098a, 16–17)

[49] https://www.oxford-review.com/oxford-review-encyclopaedia-terms/phronesis-definition-meaning/

[50] Johnson, Robert and Cureton, Adam, "Kant's Moral Philosophy," The Stanford Encyclopedia of Philosophy (Spring 2019 Edition), Edward N. Zalta (ed.) https://plato.stanford.edu/archives/spr2019/entries/kant-moral/

[51] https://www.socialigence.net/blog/difference-between-iq-eq-and-sq-the-social-intelligence-and- why-sq-is-the-future/

[52] https://www.dictionary.com/browse/empathy

[53] Schwartz, B, and Sharpe, K. (2010) Practical Wisdom: The Right Way to Do the Right Thing. Riverhead Books, N.Y. (p. 73) (Emphasis added)

[54] See the section in Chapter 4 on Understanding Human Nature

[55] https://www.britannica.com/topic/determinism

Determinism is the basis of scientific thought.

[56] https://www.theatlantic.com/magazine/archive/2016/06/theres-no-such-thing-as-free-will/480750/

[57] Described in the following chapters

[58] Facione, P. A. (1990) Critical thinking: A statement of expert consensus for purposes of educational assessment and instruction. Eric document ED315423. (p. 3).

https://files.eric.ed.gov/fulltext/ED315423.pdf

[59] Ibid.

[60] See https://serc.carleton.edu/sage2yc/self_regulated/activities.html

https://www.facultyfocus.com/articles/teaching-and-learning/what-it-means-to-be-a-self-regulated-learner/
https://www.teachermagazine.com.au/articles/teaching-

self-regulated-learning-skills

[61]https://www.nia.nih.gov/health/brain-health/cognitive-health-and-older-adults

Chapter 3

[62]Deep wisdom doesn't develop very quickly. If we're very fortunate we were born into a group of people who already practiced these metacognitive skills, so we learned them as we grew up. Otherwise, it takes a while to learn to apply them very effectively

[63]https://www.britannica.com/science/confirmation-bias

[64]The literal translation of this Greek word is "love of wisdom."

https://www.worldhistory.org/philosophy/#:~:text

https://www.philosophybasics.com/branch.html lists over a dozen branches of philosophy.

[65]https://npcassoc.org/

[66]Ennis, R. H. (1987). A taxonomy of CT skills and dispositions. In Baron, J., Sternberg, R. (Eds.), Teaching thinking skills: Theory and practice (pp. 9–26). New York, NY: W. H. Freeman. (p. 10)

[67]That is, relative to alternative perspectives

[68]Facione, P. A. (1990).

https://files.eric.ed.gov/fulltext/ED315423.pdf About half of the participants were philosophers, most of the others were educational psychologists.

[69]https://www.merriam-webster.com/dictionary/argument

[70]Dewey, J. (1939). Intelligence in the modern world. New York, NY: Random House. (p. 263).

[71]Any number of rubrics may be developed by teachers for the purpose of standardizing their assessment criteria.

[72]Hook, S. (1939). John Dewey: an intellectual portrait. Westport, Conn., Greenwood Press. (p. 39) (Emphasis added).

[73]See the section on Problem-Solving in Chapter 4

[74]https://www.sciencedirect.com/science/article/pii/B008043076700629X

[75]Boden, M. A. (1991). The creative mind: Myths & mechanisms. Basic Books

[76]Boden, M. A. (1994). What is creativity? In M. A. Boden (Ed.), Dimensions of creativity (pp. 75–117). The MIT Press. (p. 78).

[77]In 1656, Baruch (Benedict) Spinoza was excommunicated from his religious community in Amsterdam for insisting that God and Nature are identical. His notion that physical things and human experiences continually spring from one unknowable Source (Deus sive Natura: God or Nature) continues to be favored by many philosophers of religion. For more on Spinoza, see https://www.iep.utm.edu/spinoz-m/

[78] https://www.lexico.com/en/definition/fallacy

[79] https://iep.utm.edu/fallacy/#JumpingtoConclusions

[80] https://www.psychologicalscience.org/tag/cognitive-bias

[81] https://www.mentalfloss.com/article/68705/20-cognitive-biases-affect-your-decisions

[82] https://www.interaction-design.org/literature/topics/cognitive-biases

[83] https://www.ncbi.nlm.nih.gov/pubmed/10626367

[84] https://corporatefinanceinstitute.com/resources/knowledge/trading-investing/list-top-10-types-cognitive-bias/

[85] Ibid.

[86] https://www.verywellmind.com/what-is-a-cognitive-bias-2794963

[87] Ibid

[88] https://www.verywellmind.com/what-is-a-cognitive-bias-2794963

[89] https://www.verywellmind.com/what-is-the-bandwagon-effect-2795895

[90] https://www.alleydog.com/glossary/definition.php?term=Outcome%2520Bias

[91] https://www.merriam-webster.com/dictionary/halo%20effect

[92] http://www.skepdic.com/recencybias.html

[93] https://www.merriam-webster.com/dictionary/prejudice The term may also refer to any unreasonable bias in favor of a particular person or group.

[94] https://www.verywellmind.com/what-is-prejudice-2795476

Chapter 4

[95] See the section on Complex Dynamic Systems in Chapter 5

[96] https://www.merriam-webster.com/dictionary/ontology

[97] Popper, Karl (1972) Objective Knowledge: An Evolutionary Approach, Clarendon. Press: Oxford University Press.

[98] Popper, K. (1978) The Tanner Lectures on Human Values https://tannerlectures.org/wp-content/uploads/sites/105/2024/07/popper80.pdf

[99] https://poets.org/poem/harvest-moon

[100] https://science.nasa.gov/universe/dark-matter-dark-energy/

[101] For example, https://www.space.com/universe-standard-model-hubble-constant-new-measurements.html; Ultra-Large Structure Discovered in Distant Space Defies Our Current Understanding of the Universe (scitechdaily.com)

[102] https://www.universetoday.com/48619/a-universe-of-10-dimensions/

[103] As explained in Chapter 1, coherent meanings depend

on how our discourses relate to measurable events and actual practices

[104]http://www.faculty.umb.edu/gary_zabel/Courses/Marxist_Philosophy/Hegel_and_Feuerbach_files/Hegel-Phenomenology-of-Spirit.pdf

https://sites.socsci.uci.edu/~lpearl/courses/readings/BeverPoeppel2010_AnalysisBySynthesis.pdf

[105]https://dictionary.apa.org/stream-of-consciousness

[106]https://www.ncbi.nlm.nih.gov/pmc/articles/PMC2080858/

[107]See https://www.apa.org/topics/anger/control

https://www.mayoclinic.org/healthy-lifestyle/adult-health/in-depth/anger-management/art-20045434

https://www.helpguide.org/articles/relationships-communication/anger-management.htm

[108]https://www.2knowmyself.com/relationship_between_anger_and_fear

[109]https://www.psychologytoday.com/us/blog/compassion-matters/201601/should-you-feel-or-flee-your-emotions

[110]Sternberg, R.J. (1988) The triarchic mind: A new theory of human intelligence, New York: Viking Penguin. (p.169).

[111]Ibid., (p. 78)

[112]Gardner, H. (1983) Frames of Mind: The Theory of

Multiple Intelligences, New York: Basic Books. Gardner, H. (1993). Multiple Intelligences: The Theory in Practice. NY: Basic Books

[113] Salovey, Peter, and John D. Mayer. 'Emotional intelligence'. Imagination, cognition and personality, 9.3 (1989) https://journals.sagepub.com/doi/10.2190/DUGG-P24E-52WK-6CDG

[114] https://www.skillsyouneed.com/general/emotional-intelligence.html

[115] For example, see

https://managementhelp.org/personalproductivity/problem-solving.htm

[116] https://www.verywellmind.com/what-is-self-awareness-2795023

[117] Hararai, Y. N. (2018) 21 Lessons for the 21st Century, McLelland and Stewart. The Table of Contents is available at https://search.schlowlibrary.org/Record/421018/TOC

[118] https://www.budsas.org/ebud/whatbudbeliev/78.htm; http://www.middlewaysociety.org/middle-way/

[119] https://www.britannica.com/topic/golden-mean https://philosophybreak.com/articles/the-golden-mean-aristotle-guide-to-living-excellently/

[120] https://oll-resources.s3.us-east-2.amazonaws.com/oll3/store/titles/1432/0415_Bk.pdf

[121] http://www.newworldencyclopedia.org/entry/Humanism

Chapter 5

[122]Fischer, Kurt W., (1980) Psychological Review 87 (6):477–531

[123]Lipman, M. (2003) Thinking in education (2nd Ed.), Cambridge; New York: Cambridge University Press. (p. 209)

[124]Ibid., (p. 219)

[125]Halpern, D.F. (1998) Teaching critical thinking for transfer across domains, American Psychologist, 53(4), 449-455. (p. 449)

[126]Ibid., (p. 451)

[127]Paul, R. W., & Elder, L. (2002). Critical thinking: Tools for taking charge of your professional and personal life. Upper Saddle River, NJ: Pearson Education. (p. 5).

[128]Sternberg, R. J. (1987). Questions and answers about the nature and teaching of thinking skills, In J. B. Baron & R. J. Sternberg (Eds.), Teaching Thinking Skills: Theory and Practice, New York: Freeman. (pp. 251–259).

[129]Noddings, N. (2007). Philosophy of education (2nd Edition), Boulder, CO: Westview Press, p. 166.

[130]Ibid., (p. 168)

[131]https://www.thoughtco.com/cultural-hegemony-3026121

[132]Foucault, M (1975). Power/Knowledge: Selected Interviews and Other Writings 1972–1977. Pantheon. (p.

52).

[133]https://www.definitions.net/definition/critical+pedagogy

[134]Mogenson, F. (1999), "Critical thinking: a central element in developing action competence in health and environmental education," Health Education Research (12), 429–436. (p. 432).

[135]https://unesdoc.unesco.Org/ark:/48223/pf0000243126

[136]https://www.gettingsmart.com/2017/08/8-things-look-student-centered-learning-environment/

[137]https://educationaltechnology.net/vygotskys-zone-of-proximal-development-and-scaffolding/

[138]Knowles, Malcolm S. (1984) Andragogy in Action, San Francisco: Jossey Bass Publishers.

[139]Ibid., (p. 12)

[140]Ibid.

[141]https://www.britannica.com/science/cognitive-equilibrium (Emphasis added) See the section on Cognitive Equilibrium in Chapter 1.

[142]https://www.psychologytoday.com/ca/blog/the-adaptive-mind/202307/empty-your-cup-why-unlearning-is-vital-for-success

[143]Kuhn, T. S. (1962) The structure of scientific revolutions, University of Chicago Press

[144]Mezirow, J. (1991) Transformative dimensions of adult

learning, San Francisco: Jossey-Bass

[145]Érdi, P. (2008) Complexity explained, Berlin, Heidelber: Springer-Verlag.

[146]Ibid. (p. 4)

[147]McLaren, P., and Giroux, H. A. (1997) "Writing from the margins: Geographies of identity, pedagogy and power," In Peter McLaren (Ed.), Revolutionary multiculturalism: pedagogies of dissent for the new millennium, Boulder, Co.: Westview Press. (p. 16)

[148]See https://www.skillsyouneed.com/ps/reflective-practice.html

[149]Brookfield, S. D. (1995), Becoming a Critically Reflective Teacher, San Francisco: Jossey Bass. (pp. xii-xiii).

[150]Ibid., (pp. 26-27)

[151]Bruffee, K. A. (1999) Collaborative Learning: Higher Education, Interdependence, and the Authority of Knowledge, Baltimore, MD: Johns Hopkins University Press

[152]https://hbr.org/2002/03/the-anxiety-of-learning

Chapter 6

[153]https://www.forbes.com/sites/tracybrower/2023/03/19/purpose-may-be-the-key-to-happiness-3-reasons-why/

https://www.mayoclinichealthsystem.org/hometown-health/speaking-of-health/tips-for-embracing-joy-in-daily-life

[154]See https://www.health.harvard.edu/blog/how-can-you-find-joy-or-at-least-peace-during-difficult-times-202210062826
https://www.forbes.com/sites/nomanazish/2023/04/08/how-to-find-joy-in-your-everyday-life-according-to-psychologists/
https://globalnews.ca/news/9563073/cultivating-joy-how-to-bring-more-joy-into-your-daily-life/
https://www.oprahdaily.com/life/health/a32957825/how-to-find-joy/

[155]https://dictionary.cambridge.org/dictionary/english/fulfilment

[156]https://www.newworldencyclopedia.org/entry/Happiness
For an extended account of philosophical research on the subject see Haybron, Dan, 'Happiness', The Stanford Encyclopedia of Philosophy (Summer 2020 Edition), Edward N. Zalta (ed.)
https://plato.stanford.edu/archives/sum2020/entries/happiness

[157]The Art of Happiness, His Holiness The Dalai Lama and Cutler, H.C. Riverhead Books, 1998, pp. 15, 26.

[158]Maslow, A. H. (1954) Motivation and Personality, New York: Harper.

[159]Maslow, A. H. (1971), The Farther Reaches of Human Nature, New York, NY, US: Arkana/Penguin Books

[160] Doran, G. T. (1981). There's a S.M.A.R.T. Way to Write Management's Goals and Objectives. Management Review, 70, 35–36.

[161] I think of my emotions as I think of the weather conditions; they might affect how I go about my business, but (unless they're extremely powerful) they don't determine what I intend to do. As noted in Chapter 2, moral reasoning should outrank emotions when it comes to deciding what we ought to do.

[162] https://www.dalailama.com/messages/world-peace/a-human-approach-to-world-peace

[163] Epictetus. (c. 105 AD) The Discourses, Book 4.1, 174, 175

[164] See https://buddha101.com/p_path.htm#The%20Eightfold%20Path

[165] https://www.learnreligions.com/right-mindfulness-450070

[166] Brook, A. and Stainton, R.J. (2000) Knowledge and Mind: A Philosophical introduction, The MIT Press. (p.143). (Emphasis added)

[167] http://conversationsforaction.com/history/language-action-theory

[168] Ibid

[169] https://www.betterhealth.vic.gov.au/health/healthyliving/negative-emotions

[170] https://www.apa.org/topics/psychotherapy/approaches see also

https://www.mindbodygreen.com/0-17736/10-everyday-habits-to-make-you-a-calmer-person.html

[171] https://www.urmc.rochester.edu/encyclopedia/content.aspx?contenttypeid=1&contentid=2760 ; see also

https://acceleratedresolutiontherapy.com/common-psychological-emotional-problems-people-suffer-nowadays/

[172] https://www.psychologytoday.com/ca/blog/some-assembly-required/201410/moving-toward-emotional-balance

[173] https://www.psychologytoday.com/us/blog/prescriptions-life/201906/anxiety-get-over-your-fear-feeling-afraid

[174] https://psychcentral.com/blog/shame-when-youre-too-ashamed-to-talk-about-it/

https://www.yellowbrickprogram.com/blog/shame-symptoms-shame-combat

https://tinybuddha.com/blog/release-shame-stop-feeling-fundamentally-flawed/

[175] https://psychologenie.com/repression-vs-suppression-in-psychology

[176] https://www.merriam-webster.com/dictionary/cognitive%20dissonance

[177] https://www.psychologytoday.com/ca/basics/cognitive-

dissonance
https://www.verywellmind.com/what-is-cognitive-dissonance-2795012

[178]"Unity (as of a group or class) that produces or is based on community of interests, objectives, and standards" https://www.merriam-webster.com/dictionary/solidarity

[179]https://www.marxists.org/archive/marx/works/1847/11/prin-com.htm

[180]https://www.brainyquote.com/quotes/wayne_dyer_384143

[181]I've attempted to build my narrative upon the best ideas that the sages of the ages have provided. I've winnowed the field to perspectives that don't seem (to me) to contradict each other

[182]https://www.britannica.com/science/self-actualization

[183]Maslow, A. H. (1971), The Farthest Reaches of Human Nature, Penguin Compass. (p. 101).

[184]Csikszentmihalyi, M. (1990) *Flow: The Psychology of Optimal Experience,* Harper & Row.
https://blogs.baruch.cuny.edu/authenticityandastonishment2/files/2013/04/Mihaly-Csikszentmihalyi-Flow1.pdf

[185]Ibid., (p. 67–69)

[186]https://www.merriam-webster.com/dictionary/love

[187]https://www.iep.utm.edu/love-his/.

[188]https://www.psychologytoday.com/ca/blog/brainsnacks/201203/the-only-5-fears-we-all-share

[189]https://psychcentral.com/blog/nourishing-the-different-types-of-intimacy-in-your-relationship

Chapter 7

[190]https://www.therelationshipdoc.org/why-a-lack-of-tolerance-dooms-relationships/

[191]Wallace, R. Jay, "Practical Reason", The Stanford Encyclopedia of Philosophy (Spring 2020 Edition), Edward N.Zalta(ed.).

https://plato.stanford.edu/archives/spr2020/entries/practical-reason/

[192]Ibid.

[193]https://www.simplypsychology.org/defense-mechanisms.html

[194]https://www.psychologytoday.com/intl/blog/fulfillment-any-age/201711/7-things-insecure-people-do-try-seem-important

https://drjessicahiggins.com/how-to-know-if-you-are-too-critical-in-relationship-why/

https://www.psychologytoday.com/us/blog/communication-success/201807/5-ways-narcissists-compensate-for-their-inferiority

[195]https://saif-farooqi.medium.com/the-concept-of-self-

actualization-7cc2d870b353

[196]https://www.psychologytoday.com/us/blog/cutting-edge-leadership/201407/what-is-social-intelligence-why-does-it-matter

https://www.verywellmind.com/what-is-social-intelligence-4163839

[197]https://blog.mindvalley.com/interpersonal-intelligence/ See also http://www.inspiring-breakthrough.co.uk/learning-styles/interpersonal-learning.htm

https://www.ursula-sandner.com/en/can-develop-interpersonal-intelligence/

[198]To apply operationalism to the construct "social flourishing," one needs to define methods of measurement. Since there's no definitive method for operationalizing this abstraction, there may be any number of measures that one might reasonably apply.

[199]https://www.canada.ca/en/revenue-agency/corporate/careers-cra/information-moved/cra-competencies-standardized-assessment-tools.html

[200]a feeling that people have of being loyal to and proud of their country often with the belief that it is better and more important than other countries."

https://www.britannica.com/dictionary/nationalism

[201]"[T]he attitude that one's own group, ethnicity, or nationality is superior to others." https://www.merriam-

webster.com/dictionary/ethnocentrism

[202] https://www.shortform.com/blog/culturism

[203] "[U]nity (as of a group or class) that produces or is based on community of interests, objectives, and standards" https://www.merriam-webster.com/dictionary/solidarity

[204] "a belief in human equality especially with respect to social, political, and economic affairs" https://www.merriam-webster.com/dictionary/egalitarianism

[205] https://www.oxfordlearnersdictionaries.com/definition/english/cooperation

[206] Grice (1975). H. Paul Grice, Logic and Conversation. In Syntax and Semantics, Vol. 3, Speech Acts, ed. by Peter Cole and Jerry L. Morgan. New York: Academic Press, 41–58

[207] https://dictionary.cambridge.org/dictionary/english/integrity.

[208] https://plato.stanford.edu/entries/egoism/

[209] https://www.currentaffairs.org/2021/02/the-urge-to-dominate

[210] https://www.psychologytoday.com/intl/blog/theory-knowledge/201305/making-judgments-and-being-judgmental

[211] https://www.psychologytoday.com/us/blog/bringing-

[211] sex-focus/201204/whos-judmental-five-key-symptoms

[212] https://www.dictionary.com/browse/equity

[213] https://www.oxfordlearnersdictionaries.com/definition/english/fairness?q=fairness

[214] https://www.oxfordlearnersdictionaries.com/definition/english/justice

[215] Arneson, Richard, "Egalitarianism," The Stanford Encyclopedia of Philosophy (Summer 2013 Edition), Edward N. Zalta(ed.) https://plato.stanford.edu/archives/sum2013/entries/egalitarianism/

[216] https://www.oxfordlearnersdictionaries.com/definition/english/workable

[217] https://www.verywellmind.com/what-is-aggression-2794818

[218] https://www.mayoclinic.org/diseases-conditions/antisocial-personality-disorder/symptoms-causes/syc-20353928#:~:text=Overview,rights

[219] https://www.goodtherapy.org/developmental-impact-effects-shame-web-conference.html

[220] https://growcounseling.com/shame-guilt-effects/

[221] https://www.psychologytoday.com/ca/blog/anger-in-the-age-entitlement/201109/chains-resentment

[222] https://www.latimes.com/opinion/topoftheticket/la-xpm-2013-dec-06-la-na-tt-nelson-mandela-20131206-

story.html

[223] https://www.mayoclinic.org/healthy-lifestyle/adult-health/in-depth/forgiveness/art-20047692

[224] https://truthout.org/articles/the-importance-of-social-consciousness-in-an-age-of-declining-democracy/

[225] Ibid.

[226] Cooley, Charles H. (1907) The American Journal of Sociology, Volume 12. https://archive.org/details/jstor-2762377/page/n1

[227] Ibid., (p. 679)

[228] Ibid., (p. 684)

[229] https://marilynschlitz.com/cultivating-social-consciousness-2

[230] https://www.malala.org/malalas-story

[231] https://www.npr.org/2019/09/23/763452863/transcript-greta-thunbergs-speech-at-the-u-n-climate-action-summit

[232] Sternberg, R. J. (2001). Why schools should teach for wisdom: The balance theory of wisdom in educational settings. Educational Psychologist 36, 227–245.

[233] http://theconversation.com/working-together-for-critical-thinking-in-schools-41976

[234] https://www.edweek.org/teaching-learning/opinion-making-the-case-for-restoring-wisdom-to-americas-schools/2023/05

https://link.springer.com/chapter/10.1007/978-1-4020-6162-2_56

https://hub.jhu.edu/2023/03/27/david-steiner-book-wisdom-in-education/

https://www.cambridge.org/core/books/abs/cambridge-handbook-of-wisdom/educating-for-wisdom/3E27019C5681E5D8C2AE17DB146FD985